COLLECTIBLE
LANTERNS
A Price Guide

© 1997

Second Printing 1998

L-W BOOK SALES
P.O. Box 69
Gas City, IN 46933

ISBN#: 0-89538-081-1

Published by: L-W Book Sales
P.O. Box 69
Gas City, IN 46933

Please write for our free catalog.

Printed by IMAGE GRAPHICS, INC., Paducah, Kentucky

TABLE OF CONTENTS

Remarkably little change occurred in the function and design of the oil lamp since Ancient Roman times until the late 18th Century. The kerosene lantern changed all this, however, with a new readily available fuel that burned longer, brighter, and more efficiently. In the 1700s, many oil and petroleum seeps were located within Pennsylvania yet could not be economically collected and refined until the mid-1850s. From 1700 to 1800 over 500 American patents were issued for improvements in lighting devices. In 1861 Colonel Drake found great fortune when his first "spouter" of crude oil broke through and others soon followed with newly discovered reservoirs. By 1866, 194 distilleries were operating in the United States with a yearly output of 28 million gallons. (With kerosene came new designs of lanterns and burners better suited for the more volatile material, and lighting by flame lamp (as opposed to candlelight and lard oils) reached its peak.) Almost all at once, other lamp oils besides kerosene became obsolete. The common kerosene burner was acknowledged as having a flat wick, a spur turn-up, a dome shaped deflector with a chimney, and a draft deflector and improved font being the most important new features.

The lanterns illustrated within this book were readily available in stores throughout the nation, and the railroad lanterns were ordered directly from manufacturers by the railroad companies themselves, somewhat limiting availability to non-employees.

All of the catalog pages included within are dated the year the lanterns were sold, not the year of manufacture. If you would like to date your lanterns, a book we would recommend for this purpose is *Lanterns That Lit Our World* by Anthony Hobson – available (for $14.95 plus $2.00 shipping) from L-W Book Sales, P.O. Box 69, Gas City, IN 46933.

PRICING INFORMATION

There are certain characteristics to look for in pricing a lantern. One is the type or usage. For instance a maritime or inspector's lantern will probably bring a higher price than your ordinary barn or tubular lanterns, because of the overabundance of manufacturing. The color of the globe is another good way of determining the value of a lantern. In most cases a colored globe (Ruby, Blue or Green, etc.) are rarer then your common clear globe.

The values in this book should be used only as a guide. These prices may vary from one region of the country to another. All prices are also affected by the condition as well as the demand of the lantern. The publisher does not assume responsibility for any gains or losses that might be incurred as a result of using this guide.

The values listed in this book have been arrived at by monitoring sale prices of lanterns within classifieds and other antique / collectible magazine advertisements, collector's shows, antique dealers, and antique malls, with an occasional glimpse of auction results as well.

REFERENCE MATERIALS ETC.

The following titles are old merchandise catalogs which proved immensely useful in the research of this book.

* Various general line merchandise catalogs
* "Adlake Signal Lamps & Lanterns" 1907 catalog
* "Adams & Westlake Company Bulletin Binder" 1911-1922
* Maritime 1909 catalog
* "Signaling" 1894

ACKNOWLEDGMENTS

L-W Book Sales & Publishing would like to issue a special "thank you" to the following individuals for helping make this project a success.

Howard Johnson (Marion, Indiana)

Gwen Goldman: Gwen's Antiques
                  P.O. Box 936
                  Adamstown, PA 19501

DIETZ LANTERNS

Referring to the dates listed with each lantern, these lanterns were sold in that year and afterwards.

Boat Lantern.

Station Lantern.

240.

Hexagon Taper Lantern.

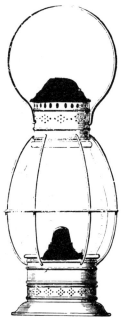

Hand Lantern.

Hand Lantern.

242.

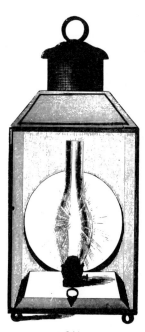

241.

(These Lanterns can be used in out-buildings or the open air.)

Excelsior Hand Lantern, showing the proper
size of the flame when burning.

Boat Lantern.

Sugar House Lantern.

Street Lantern.

184   LANTERNS.

POLICE BULL'S EYE.
In Tin . . . .
In Brass . . . .
For lard and sperm oil.

RAIL ROAD.
Single Guard . . . .
Double "   the Strongest
and Best, ...

BRILLIANT.
The most convenient coal oil lantern for family use . . . .

STATION OR FACTORY LAMPS.
No. 1, 8x12 in., 5/8 in. Wick . . .
No. 2, 10x14 in., 1 in. Wick . . . .
No. 3, 12x16 in., 1 in. Wick . . . .
With Silvered Glass Reflector.

THE BOSS.
Tubular . . . .

LITTLE BOSS.
Tubular, Tin . . . .
   "   Brass . . . .

Coal Oil, Candle and Oil Lanterns, Tubular Street Lamps, Pocket and Small Brass
Lanterns of many kinds.   Conductors' Lanterns, Nickel Plated.
Red and Blue Lantern Globes.

HEADQUARTERS FOR TORCHES AND CAMPAIGN
GOODS.

Our stock is most complete in this line, when there is a demand for these goods. Write for Prices.
During the campaigns we will issue a list of the different styles kept by us in stock.

VAJEN & NEW, INDIANAPOLIS, IND.

STATION LAMPS.

Nos. 11, 21 and 31.　　　　Nos. 22 and 34.　　　　Nos. 12, 23 and 33.　　　　No. 4.

No. 11–Square, blue, 8×10   in., height 15½ in., ⅝ in. burner, ⅝ in. wick, 7 in. silvered reflector, -　each $2.50
No. 21–Square, blue, 10×12   in., height 17½ in., 1 in. burner, 1 in. wick, 8 in. silvered reflector, -　"　 3.00
No. 31–Square, blue, 11×15½ in., height 21   in., 1 in. burner, 1 in. wick, 10 in. silvered reflector, -　"　 3 50
No. 22–Triangular, blue, 10×11 in., height 18¼ in., 1 in. burner, 1 in. wick, 8 in. silvered reflector, -　"　 3.00
No. 34–Triangular, blue, 12×14 in , height 18¼ in., 1 in. burner, 1 in. wick, 10 in. silvered reflector, -　"　 3.50
No. 12–Square tubular, blue, height 19   in., No. 2 burner, 1   in. wick, 6 in. silvered reflector,　-　"　 5.50
No. 23–Square tubular, blue, height 21½ in., No. 3 burner, 1½ in. wick, 8 in. silvered reflector,　-　"　 6.50
No. 33–Square tubular, blue, height 26   in., No. 3 burner, 1½ in. wick, 12 in. silvered reflector,　-　"　 8.50
No. 4–Triangular tubular. blue, height 22 in., No. 3 burner, 1½ in. wick. 10 in. silvered reflector,　"　 8.50

ONE IN A CASE.

SIDE LAMPS AND HEADLIGHTS.

No. 15.　　　　No. 17.

No. 634.

No. 15 –Tubular side lamps, blue, ⅝ in. burner, ⅝ in. wick, No. 0 globe, 5 in. silvered reflector, per dozen $18.00
No. 17 –Tubular side lamps, blue, 1 in. burner, 1 in wick, No. 0 globe, 6 in. silvered reflector,　"　　22.00
No. 634–Motor headlights, extreme height 22 in., 10 in. silvered copper reflector, dash board attachment for
　　cable or motor car, ·　·　·　·　·　·　·　·　·　·　·　·　·　·　each　17.00

Nos. 15 AND 17, HALF DOZEN ; No 634, ONE IN A CASE.

TUBULAR DASH LANTERNS.

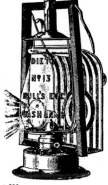

Nos. 297 and 299.　　　　　　　　　　No. 215.

No. 297–Bright tin, corrugated reflector, ⅝ in. burner, ⅝ in. wick, No. 0 globe, without bull's eye lens, top
lift, • • • • • • • • • • • • • • • • per dozen $ 9.50

No. 299–Japanned, with bull's eye lens attached to perforated plate, otherwise same as No. 299, " 10.50

No. 215–Bright tin hood 6 in. deep, 5 in. silvered glass reflector, ⅝ in. burner, ⅝ in wick, No. 0 globe, top
lift, • • • • • • • • • • • • • • • • • • per dozen 22.00

HALF DOZEN IN A CASE.

DRIVING LAMPS.　　　　SEARCHLIGHTS

No. 18.　　　　　　No. 354.

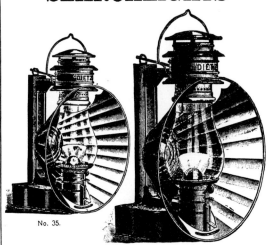

No. 35.

No. 40.

No. 18–Ham's tubular, japanned, height 9½ in.,
weight 2 lbs., 4 in. double convex lens, silvered reflector, ruby rear lights, with bail
and wire spring fastening, also separate
clamp for side of dash, ⅜ in. wick, per doz. $42.00

No. 354–Dietz tubular, japanned, height 11 in.,
5 in. beveled plate glass front, spring at
back to attach to dash, also detachable
holder fitting right or left side of dash and
screw holder for flat surfaces, ⅜ in. wick,
per doz • • • • • • • • 42.00

HALF DOZEN IN A CASE.

No. 35–Tubular, blued tin, 1 in. burner, 1 in.
wick, No. 0 globe, 12×7 in. tin reflector,
per doz. • • • • • • • $30.00

No. 40–Tubular, blued tin, 1½ in. wick, 1½ in
burner, No. 2 globe, 20×10 in. tin reflector,
per doz. • • • • • • • 72.00

NO. 35 QUARTER DOZEN ; NO. 40 ONE IN A CASE.

GLOBE TUBULAR LAMPS.

No. 97.
For No. 3 and No. 30 lamps.

Nos. 30 and D30.

Nos. 3 and D3.

No.   30—Painted green. hanging, with bottom lift, No. 3 burner, 1½ in wick, No. 3 globe, height 22 in., each $6.00
No. D30—Same as No. 30, with glass fount,   ·   ·   ·   ·   ·   ·   "   6.50
No.   3—Painted green, for post, with bottom lift, No. 3 burner, 1½ in. wick, No. 3 globe, height 27 in., " 6.00
No.   D3=Same as No. 3, with glass fount, ·   ·   ·   ·   ·   ·   ·   "   6.50
No.   96—Fount and burner, with time regulator and glass oil reservoir, as above, ·   ·   "   2.50
No.   97—Same as No. 96, all tin, ·   ·   ·   ·   ·   ·   ·   ·   "   2.00

Can be set to burn a certain number of hours. and then goes out. Have outside wick regulator. Will not blow out.

ONE IN A CASE.

No. 55.

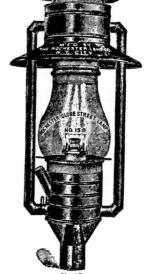

No 65.

No. 55—Rochester, hanging, painted green, with No. 2 Rochester chimney and No. 3 tubular globe, height
    with bail, 26½ in., ·   ·   ·   ·   ·   ·   ·   ·   ·   ·   ·   each $10.00
No. 65—Rochester, street, painted green, with No. 2 Rochester chimney, No 3 tubular globe, height 31 in., "   10.00

The lamps are protected by metal gauze against insects or bugs. No flickering light. Gives three times the light of flat wick lamp.

ONE IN A CASE.

TUBULAR LANTERNS.

No. 110–Top lift, No. 0 globe, ⅝ in. burner,
⅝ in. wick, · · · · per doz. $7.50
ONE DOZEN IN A CASE.

No. 242–Side lift, No. 0 globe, ⅝ in. burner,
⅝ in. wick, · · · per doz. $7.50
ONE DOZEN IN A CASE.

No. 249–Swing, No. 0 globe, ⅝ in. burner,
⅝ in. wick, · · · per doz. $7.50
ONE DOZEN IN A CASE.

No. 243–Side lift, large fount, No. 0 globe,
1 in. burner. 1 in. wick, · · per doz. $10.00
ONE DOZEN IN A CASE.

No. 244–Anti-friction, No 0 globe, ⅝ in. burner
⅝ in. wick, · · · per doz $9.00
ONE DOZEN IN A CASE

No. 363–Side lift, guarded glass fount, No. 0
globe, ⅝ in. burner, ⅝ in. wick, per doz. $10.00
No. 3630–Glass founts for No. 363 lanterns,
per doz · · · · · 3.00
ONE DOZEN IN A CASE.

TUBULAR LANTERNS.

No. 7-Regular, No. 0 globe, ⅝ in. burner, ⅝ in. wick, - - - - - per doz. $7 00
ONE DOZEN IN A CASE.

No. 8-Railroad pattern, No. 39 R. R. globe, ⅜ in. burner, ⅜ in. wick, - - per doz. $13.00
ONE DOZEN IN A CASE.

No. 258-Top litt, round frame, extra large frame and fount, No. 1 globe, 1 in. burner, 1 in. wick, - - - - per doz. $16.00
ONE DOZEN IN A CASE.

No. 211-U. S. brass, U. S. globe, ⅜ in. burner, ⅜ in. wick, - - - - per doz. $12.00
No. 212-U. S. brass, nickel plated, otherwise same as No. 211, - - per doz. 18.00
ONE DOZEN IN A CASE.

CANDLE LANTERNS.

No. 2-Cold blast, round frame, No. 0 globe, 1 in. burner, 1 in. wick, - - per doz. $14.50
ONE DOZEN IN A CASE.

No. 50-Dandy, without chimney or candle (for No. 2 Sun chimney), - - per doz..$3.00
TWO DOZEN IN A BOX.

"Dietz" Side Lift or Victor Tubular Lantern.

For Kerosene. Our 46c Lantern has no equal for the money. Over 8,000 sold last year.

No. 77503 This is the most popular Lantern on the market today.

The crank at the side raises and lowers the globe and locks the burner in place when down. A late improvement on this lantern consists of a bend on the guard wire over which the crank moves, thus perfectly locking the globe frame and burner down.

No. 1 burner, ⅝-inch wick. No. O globe. Weight, about 2 lbs.

Price, each.... ....$0.46

"Dietz" Crystal Tubular Lantern.

For Kerosene. 62c Buys a $1.00 Lantern.

No. 77505 This is a strongly guarded tubular lantern with a glass fount instead of tin. This enables the user to see how much oil is in the fount, and the fount will never leak. Fitted with our improved side lift. While the fount on this lamp is strongly guarded and is not liable to breakage, still in case of accidentally breaking it can easily be removed and a new one put in. No. 1 burner, ⅝-inch wick, No. O globe. Weight, about 2½ lbs. Price, each..........$0.62

"Deitz" U. S. Brass and Nickel Plated Tubular Lantern.

At 65c and 97c we offer the handsomest Lantern of the kind ever made. You would pay your local merchant $1.00 to $1.50 for the same lantern.

WE MAKE ONE PRICE TO YOU, the actual cost to make, with but one small profit added. For Kerosene.

No. 77510 This is the smallest tubular lantern we make. Made of brass, very handsome. For use around the house and for ladies' use it cannot be excelled. No. O burner, ⅝-inch wick, U. S. globe, weight, 1¼ lbs. Price, each 65c

No. 77511 Same as above, nickel plated. Price, each............97c

"Dietz" No. IB Side Lift Tubular Lantern.

A SPECIAL BARGAIN at 59c and such a lantern as your local merchant would charge you at least $1.00 for.

For Kerosene.

No. 77513 This Lantern has the No. 2 Burner, 1-inch Wick, and should fill a want where a large amount of light is needed in a hand lantern. The oil pot holds 1¼ pints of oil, and the lantern will burn 19 hours without refilling.

No. 2   1-Inch   No.
Burner   Wick   O Globe
Weight, about 2 lbs.
Price, each...... .....$0.59

"Dietz" Safety Tubular Mill Lantern

97c For a Regular $1.75 Lantern.

For Kerosene.

No. 77516 The Burner is locked in place by two positive locks on globe frame, which work automatically. In addition to this a padlock may be used to secure the globe frame and the guard frame permanently, if desired.

The Guard has our patent wind break, which prevents access to the flame over the top of the globe. It is extra strong, well made, and is locked in position by an automatic spring.

The Base of the lantern is given extra strength, and is locked permanently to the frame by the use of our patent side braces, holding them firmly together, independent of solder, a feature not found in any other make of lanterns. The combustion of the lantern being perfect, it burns with a clear white flame, gives a brilliant light, and the oil never heats.

The Oil Fount is large, holding 1¼ pints of oil, and the lantern will burn 19 hours without refilling.

The Lantern is substantially made in every way, with a solid drawn, retinned oil fount.

This Lantern has been endorsed by insurance men wherever shown as the safest kerosene burning lantern made.

Improved burner. ⅝-inch wick. No. O globe.

Per doz., $11.25; each 97c

"Dietz" Square Lift Brass Tubular Fire Department Lantern.

$3.00 to $5.00 is the price at which this lantern is sold in cities. UNQUESTIONABLY THE BEST LANTERN manufactured, and offered by us for $2.28. WE WILL SAVE YOU one-half in price.

For Kerosene.

No. 77518 This is a good, strong lantern, made of heavy polished brass and fitted with our patent wind break guard. Our Fire Department Lanterns have all our latest improvements. Are made extra heavy, with large double oil pots. Adopted by the American Fire Engine Companies in the principal fire departments and insurance patrols in the United States. No. 1 burner. ⅝-inch wick. No. O globe. Price, each.............$2.28

"Dietz" Buckeye or No. 13 Tubular Side and Dash Lamp.

Our Special 65c Buckeye Dash Lantern.

No. 77520 This is really a very handy combination; it serves as a hand lantern and a side or dash lamp. We furnish it japanned blue. The lamp can be fastened under the body of the vehicle by means of a holder. (See No. 77540). We furnish this lamp with our new bull's eye lens—a bull's eye attached to the perforated plate. It is superior in every way to the bull's eye globe. No. 1 burner, ⅝-inch wick, No. O globe; weight, about 2½ lbs. Price, per doz., $7.40; each.............65c

"Dietz" Tubular Driving Lamp.

(Patented.)

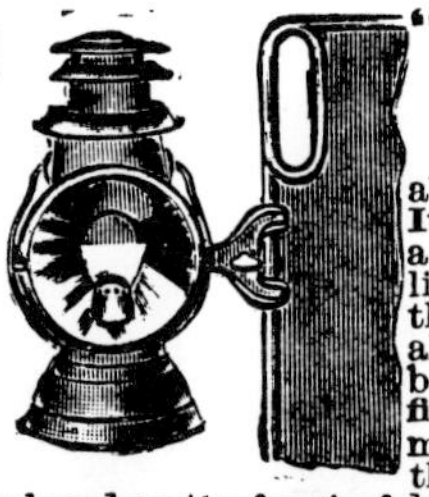

No. 77535 It is a practicable and perfect driving lamp. It will not blow out; it gives a clear, white light; it looks like a locomotive headlight; it throws all the light straight ahead from 200 to 300 feet; it burns kerosene. Handsomely finished; japanned. By means of a spring on the back the lamp can be instantly placed on the front of dash: by means of the holder it can be attached to either side of the dash. It can also be placed on the bracket of a carriage. 11 inches high; 6 inches in diameter. Weight, 2¼ lbs.

Price, each, japanned......................$2.32

"Dietz" Tubular Hunting Lamp.

No. 77536 Looks like a locomotive headlight. It will not blow nor jar out. The hood over the front works perfectly and without noise; when the hood is down no light escapes. It will throw a powerful light 200 feet. It burns kerosene oil and will burn ten hours without refilling. It is compact and handsome. Has a bail and can be used as a hand and wall lantern in camp. Gives a brilliant light, and is absolutely safe. 11 inches high; 6 inches in diameter. Weight, 2¼ lbs. Price, each....$2.79

Lantern Holders.

No. 77540 Warner Tubular Lantern Holder. For holding a tubular lantern under the body of a wagon for night driving.

Price, each................20c

Bull's Eye Lens.

No. 77541 Bull's Eye Lens. Attached to perforated plate. For all tubular lanterns taking No. O (the common size) globe. Takes the place of bull's eye globes at little expense; no danger of breakage and better in every way. Each......15c

"Dietz" New Farm Lantern.

For Oil, Candle or Kerosene.

No. 77545 A Cheap, Square Lantern. If glass should get broken, a light of 7x9 window glass, cut in three equal pieces, forms three lights for the sides. Each lantern has a burner for oil, one for kerosene, and a candleholder, all furnished with lantern without extra charge. Weight, 1½ lbs. Price, each..............$0.35 Price, per doz..... ...3.67

Wire Bottom R. R. Lantern.

No. 77548 There are no better Railroad Lanterns made than ours. The bail is made so that when the lantern is put down the bail stands up. It is the strongest railroad lantern on the market. Hinge top, removable globe, wire bottom, casts no shadow, bail fast to guard bayonet catch on oil pot. Weighs 2½ lbs. Burns Lard Oil. Price, per doz., $5.40; each..50c

Dietz Tubular Driving Lamp.

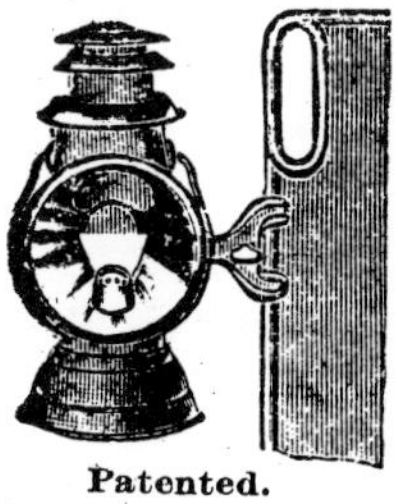

Patented.

No. 23V7040 It is a practicable and perfect driving lamp. It will not blow out; it gives a clear, white light; it looks like a locomotive headlight; it throws all the light straight ahead; it burns kerosene. Handsomely finished; japanned. By means of a spring on the back, the lamp can be instantly placed on the front of dash; by means of the holder it can be attached to either side of the dash. It can also be placed on the bracket of a carriage. 11 inches high; 6 inches in diameter. Weight, 2½ pounds.
Price, japanned........................**$2.10**

Dietz Tubular Hunting Lamp.

No. 23V7045 Looks like a locomotive headlight. It will not blow nor jar out. The hood over the front works perfectly and without noise; when the hood is down no light escapes. It will throw a powerful light. It burns kerosene oil and will burn ten hours without refilling. It is compact and handsome. Has a bail and can be used as a hand and wall lantern in camp. Gives a brilliant light, and is absolutely safe. 11 inches high; 6 inches in diameter. Weight 2½ pounds.
Price.................**$3.00**

Lantern Holder.

No. 23V7052 Warner Tubular Lantern Holder. For holding a tubular lantern under the body of a wagon for night driving. Weight, 6 ounces. Price..**20c**

Bull's-Eye Lens.

No. 23V7055 Bull's-Eye Lens. Attached to perforated plate. For all tubular lanterns taking No. 0 (the common size) globe Takes the place of bull's-eye globes at little expense; no danger of breakage and better in every way. Weight, 4 ounces. Price.......**10c**

Dietz New Farm Lantern.

For Oil, Candle or Kerosene.

No. 23V7060 A cheap, square lantern. If glass should get broken, a light of 7x9 window glass, cut in three equal pieces, forms three lights for the sides. Each lantern has a burner for oil, one for kerosene, and a candleholder, all furnished with lantern without extra charge. Weight, 1½ pounds. Price..........**40c**

10-Inch Square Traction Engine Headlight.

No. 23V7150 This Headlight is especially adapted for Traction Engines, as it gives a very strong light, and the draft is so arranged that the flame will not smoke or blow out in high winds, nor jar out in passing over rough roads. Packed complete with attachments to fit to engine. Weight, crated, 30 pounds.
Price.....................................**$6.50**

Dietz Square Station Lamp.

Packed one each in a case, complete with fount, burner, chimney and silvered glass reflector.

No. 23V7162 8x10 inches; has No. 1 burner, ⅝-inch wick, 7-inch silvered glass reflector. Weight, packed for shipment, 15 lbs. Price.**$1.67**

No. 23V7163 10x12 inches; has No. 2 burner, 1-inch wick, 8-inch silvered glass reflector. Weight, packed for shipment, 20 pounds. Price........................**$1.93**

No. 23V7164 11x15½ inches; has No. 2 burner, 1-inch wick, 10-inch silvered glass reflector. Weight, packed for shipment, 25 pounds.
Price.....................................**$2.20**

Dietz R. R. Lantern.

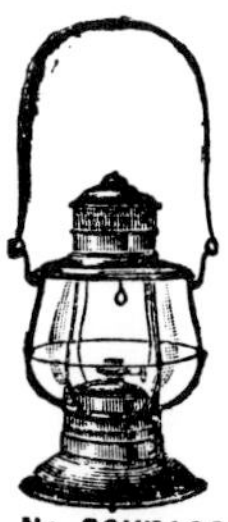

No. 23V7092 Conductors' or Railroad Lantern. Made of brass, nickel plated; bail fastened to the guard. The bails are made so that when the lantern is put down the bail stands up. Hinged top and removable globe. Weight, 2¼ pounds.
Price..................**$2.35**

Car Inspectors' Lantern.

No. 23V7100 Car Inspectors' Lantern. This lantern is used by car inspectors. It throws a powerful light to a distance. It has a 5-inch silvered glass reflector. which will never tarnish, and a 5-inch beveled glass bull's-eye. Takes 1-inch wick, burns kerosene. It is an excellent lantern for rough usage. Weight, 3 pounds. Price.............. ....**$2.00**

Police or Dark Lanterns.

No. 23V7125
No. 23V7100

No. 23V7125 Police or Dark Lanterns, 2¾-inch bull's-eye. Weight, 12 ounces. **Burns Sperm Oil.** Price............**31c**

No. 23V7126 Police Lanterns, 3-inch bull's-eye. Weight, 16 ounces.
Price................**34c**

No. 23V7130
No. 32V7132

No. 23V7130 Special quality dark lanterns, made of heavy tin, nickel plated, finest finish and strongest in the market; furnished with the best quality fire polished lens. Weight, each, 14 ounces, with 2½-inch lens. Price...................**90c**

No. 23V7131 With 3-inch lens. Weight, 18 ounces. Price.............................**$1.13**

No. 23V7132 Same as No. 23V7130, but is made of polished brass, with 2½-inch lens.
Price.......................................**$1.88**

No. 23V7133 With 3-inch lens. Price, **2.47**

Dietz Tubular Side Lamps.

No. 23V7145 These Lamps operate on the same principle as our tubular lanterns, and are not affected by wind; never heat, and are perfectly safe. Can be lit, filled and regulated without removing the globe. They are japanned blue, and are unsurpassed for use in shops, halls and factories. Have 1-inch burner and wick, No. 0 globe, and 6-inch silvered glass reflector. Weight, 2 pounds.
Price..............**$1.10**

Dietz Search Light.

No. 23V7148 For outdoor or indoor use. Will not blow out. Gives a powerful and brilliant light. Simple and effective device for raising globe, for lighting and trimming. No. 2 burner, 1-inch wick, No. 0 globe. Weight, 3¾ pounds.
Price, **$1.50**

Dietz Improved Tubular Lamp.

No chimney. Improved burner. Does not smoke. Outside wick regulator. Light equal to gas, at a less cost. Will not blow out in the strongest wind; brilliant light. Packed, one each, in a case.

No. 23V7170 Has No. 2 burner, 1-inch wick, 6-inch silvered glass reflector. Weight, packed for shipment, 16 pounds. Height, 19 inches.
Price........................**$3.30**

No. 23V7171 Has No. 3 burner, 1½-inch wick, 8-inch silvered glass reflector. Weight, packed for shipment, 23 pounds. Height, 21½ inches. Price...**$3.89**

No. 23V7172 Has No. 3 burner, 1½-inch wick, 12-inch silvered glass reflector. Weight, packed for shipment, 40 pounds. Height, 26 inches. Price.............................**$5.13**

Dietz Tubular Hanging Street Lamp.

No. 23V7180 Will not blow out in the strongest wind. No chimney, new globe lifter, improved burner, outside wick regulator, automatic extinguisher, does not smoke. Light equal to gas, at a less cost. Is useful wherever a strong light is desired. Has No. 2 burner, 1-inch wick, No. 2 globe. Weight, packed for shipment, 23 pounds.
Price......................**$3.08**

No. 23V7181 Globe Tubular Hanging Lamp. Same style as above. Has No. 3 burner, 1½-inch wick, No. 3 globe. Can be regulated to burn a certain number of hours. Has automatic extinguisher. Weight, packed for shipment, 31 pounds.
Price...**$3.38**

No. 23V7182 Globe Tubular Hanging Lamp. Same as No. 23V7181, except it has glass fount.
Price...**$3.53**

Dietz Corporation Street Lamp.

No. 23V7191 This Lamp is fitted with a glass oil fount, kerosene burner and chimney, and has a removable cast iron socket that will fit a post or bracket. The upper part of lamp is removable and they nest close for shipment. Packed one in each case. Average weight, with case, 40 pounds. Net, with socket, 15 pounds. Height, 32¼ inches. No. 2 burner. 1-inch wick. No. 2 Sun chimney. Price.....................**$2.95**

Dietz No. 2 Square Tubular Lamp.

For Kerosene.

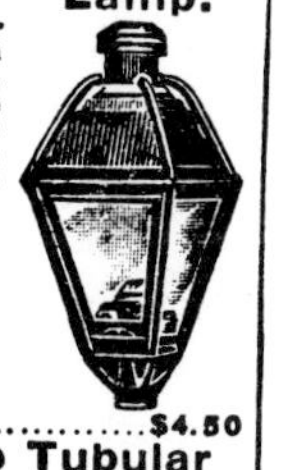

No. 23V7194 No Chimney. Light equal to gas at a less cost. Brilliant flame. Will not blow out in the strongest wind. Automatic extinguisher. Can be regulated to burn a certain number of hours. Warranted to give satisfaction. This is a very large and handsome lamp. For lamp in front of lodge room, store or church it cannot be excelled. No. 3 burner, 1½-inch wick, 3-inch flame. Weight, packed for shipment, 43 pounds. Price.............................**$4.50**

Dietz No. 3 Globe Tubular Street Lamp.

No. 23V7196 Warranted to give perfect satisfaction. More sold than all other makes combined. No chimney. Light equal to gas at a less cost. New globe lifter. Outside wick regulator. Does not smoke. Casts no shadow. Will not blow out in the strongest wind. Can be regulated to burn a certain number of hours. This lamp never fails to give perfect satisfaction. It can be filled, lighted and regulated without removing the globe. The reflector is painted white and the lamp painted green. Packed one each in a case, measuring 3¾ cubic feet. Average weight with case, 30 pounds; net 9¼ pounds; 27 inches high; No. 3 burner; 1½-inch wick; No. 3 globe. Price.........................**$3.38**

Wire Bottom R. R. Lantern.
Burns Lard Oil.

No. 23V7069 There are no better railroad lanterns made than ours. The bail is made so that when the lantern is put down the bail stands up. It is the strongest railroad lantern on the market. Hinge top, removable globe, wire bottom, casts no shadow, bail fastened to guard. Bayonet catch on oil pot. Weight, 2½ pounds. Price.........57c

Tin Bottom R. R. Lantern.
Standard size; burns Lard Oil.

No. 23V7070 Bail fastened to the guard. The bails are made so that when the lantern is put down the bail stands up. Hinged top and removable globe. There are no better railroad lanterns made than ours. Weight, 2 pounds. Price......58c

Dietz Conductors' Lantern.
Burns Lard Oil.

No. 23V7075 Conductors' Lantern is made of brass, finely finished and nickel plated. Has hinged top, removable globe, ⅝-inch ratchet burner. Plain flint globe. Weight, 2½ pounds.

Price	$4.00
Add for half green or half blue globe	1.47
Half ruby, add	1.50
Add for engraving name on globe	.75
Name with wreath	1.00

No. 23V7090 Plain Crystal Globe to fit above conductors' lantern; they are hand made, from the best lead glass. Weight, 2½ pounds. Price..................40c

TUBULAR LANTERNS.

We illustrate all the latest designs and our lanterns have the latest improvements. We show a larger variety to select from. They are safe and reliable. While our prices are lower than formerly, we still maintain our superior quality.

In selecting a lantern you should aim to secure the safest and best. Remember there are some makes of cheap lanterns that cause much annoyance as well as damage. The difference in price between our lanterns, the very best, and inferior makes is but a few cents.

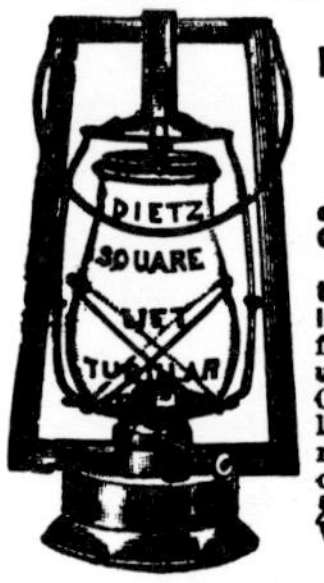

Dietz Square Lift, or Star Tubular Lantern.
For Kerosene.

Our 45c lantern has no equal for the money. Over 8,000 sold last year.
No. 23V7000 This is the old reliable square lift lantern. We have sold it for years, and it gives universal satisfaction. One of our most popular lanterns. The globe is raised by the thumb piece on top. No. 1 burner, ⅝-inch wick. No. 0 globe. Weight, about 1¾ pounds. Price................45c

Dietz Side Lift or Victor Tubular Lantern.
For Kerosene.

No. 23V7002 This is the most popular lantern on the market today. The crank at the side raises and lowers the globe and locks the burner in place when down. A late improvement on this lantern consists of a bend on the guard wire over which the crank moves, thus perfectly locking the globe frame and burner down. No. 1 burner, ⅝-inch wick. No. 0 globe. Weight, about 1¾ lbs. Price 45c

Dietz Crystal Tubular Lantern.

No. 23V7005 This is a strongly guarded tubular lantern with a glass fount instead of tin. This enables the user to see how much oil is in the fount, and the fount will never leak. Fitted with our improved side lift. While the fount on this lantern is strongly guarded and is not liable to breakage, still in case of accidentally breaking it can easily be removed and a new one put in. No. 1 burner; ⅝-inch wick; No. 0 globe. Weight, about 2½ pounds. Price...62c

Dietz No. 1B Side Lift Tubular Lantern.
For Kerosene.

No. 23V7012 This Lantern has the No. 2 burner, 1-inch wick, and should fill a want where a large amount of light is needed in a hand lantern. The oil pot holds 1¾ pints of oil, and the lantern will burn nineteen hours without refilling. No. 2 burner, 1-inch wick. No. 0 globe. Weight, about 2 lbs. Price..62c

Dietz Junior Cold Blast Lantern.

No. 23V7016 Only 12 inches high and gives a light equal to many lanterns double its size. It can be filled, lighted, regulated and extinguished without removing the globe. It burns on the cold blast principle, taking most of its air supply from above the globe and will not blow out in the strongest wind. Our Junior Cold Blast possesses all the advantages of our regular No. 2 cold blast lantern, but in more compact form, and is unequaled where a light, handy lantern is required. Price 60c

No. 23V7018 Dietz Junior Cold Blast Lantern, same as No. 23V7016, except it is made of brass, highly polished. Price................90c

No. 23V7019 Dietz Junior Cold Blast Lantern, same as No. 23V7016, except it is made of brass and is highly polished and nickel plated. Price..................................$1.10

Dietz Safety Tubular Mill Lantern.

No. 23V7017 The burner is locked in place by two positive locks on globe frame, which work automatically. In addition to this a padlock may be used to secure the globe frame and the guard frame permanently, if desired. The guard has our patent wind break, which prevents access to the flame over the top of the globe. The oil fount holds 1¾ pints of oil, will burn 19 hours without refilling, has a solid drawn, retinned oil fount. This lantern has been endorsed by insurance men wherever shown as the safest kerosene burning lantern made. Improved burner, ⅝-inch wick. No. 0 globe. Weight, 2½ pounds. Price..... .. .90c

Dietz Square Lift Brass Tubular Fire Department Lantern.
For Kerosene.

No. 23V7020 This is a good, strong lantern, made of heavy polished brass and fitted with our patent wind break guard. Our Fire Department Lanterns have all our latest improvements. Are made extra heavy, with large double oil pots. Adopted by the American fire engine companies in the principal fire departments and insurance patrols in the United States. No. 1 burner. ⅝-inch wick. No. 0 globe. Weight, 3 lbs. Price..............$1.95

Dietz Buckeye or No. 13 Tubular Side and Dash Lantern.

No. 23V7025 This is really a very handy combination; it serves as a hand lantern and a side or dash lamp. The lamp can be fastened under the body of the vehicle by means of a holder. (See No. 23V7052.) We furnish this lamp with our new bull's-eye lens—a bull's eye attached to the perforated plate. It is superior in every way to the bull's-eye globe. No. 1 burner, ⅝-inch wick, No. 0 globe. Weight, about 2¾ pounds.
Price.........68c

Dietz No. 0 Reflector Tubular Lantern.
For Kerosene.

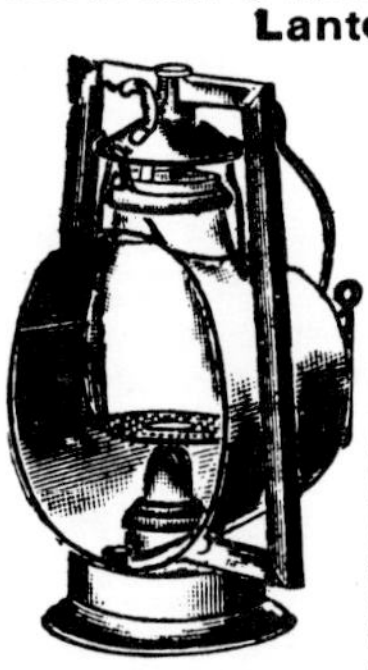

No. 23V7027 The globe can be raised for lighting. The hood is 6 inches deep, fitted with a 5-inch silvered glass reflector and a spring fastening for dash. Can also be used as a hand lantern or wall lamp. It is a desirable lantern for night driving and will throw a strong light over 100 feet. We have never heard of one of them blowing or jarring out. The lamp can be fastened under the body of the vehicle by means of our Warner holders (See No. 23V7052.) No. 1 long cone burner, ⅝-inch wick, No. 0 globe. Weight, about 2¾ pounds. Price.........$1.10

Cold Blast Dash Lamp.

No. 23V7030 Cold Blast Dash Lamp. No. 2 burner, 1-inch wick, No. 0 globe. This lamp is intended for use when a very powerful light is required. It will not blow out in the strongest wind, and does not flicker as much as a lantern without windbreak. We furnish this lantern japanned blue. Weight, 2¾ pounds. Price.......$1.00

Dietz Junior Cold Blast Dash Lantern.

No. 23V7031 This is our Junior Cold Blast Lantern with dash attachment and corrugated reflector added. It is wind proof, easy to regulate, and gives a brilliant light, and is a first class lamp for night driving and for the stable. Weight, 1½ pounds. Price, 75c

Cold Blast Driving Lamp.

Dietz "Monarch" Lanterns

Dietz "Monarch" lantern is one of the most popular lanterns ever made. Bright tin construction. Has all the latest improvements, including positive-locking globe lift on inside of frame, large oil filler, and patent safety wing lock burner, dome-shaped solderless oil fount, reinforced tubes and security standing bail hooked into patent brass eyelets. For kerosene, wicked ready for lighting. Has No. 1 "Victor" tinned steel burner; size of wick, ⅝ inches. Height over all, 13⅝ inches. Wt., 2 lbs...........$ .45
Extra globes, white, $ .06; red, $ .20; bull's eye, $ .15.

Deitz U. S. Lanterns

A small lantern suitable for women or boys. Especially desirable for getting illumination for parades, etc. This lantern is 10 inches high, has ⅝-inch wick and burns kerosene 14 hours without refilling. Made in assorted colors, lacquered on tin. Wicked ready to use. Wt., 1 lb. ....$ .35

Dietz "Junior" Lantern

The Dietz "Junior" kerosene cold blast lantern is the best selling of all similar lanterns. It is of a handy size, gives a remarkable light for a small lantern (6 c. p.) and has all the latest improvements—globe lift inside of frame, patent safety wing-lock burner, security standing bail hooked into patent brass eyelets, dome-shaped solderless oil fount, etc. Has patented No. 1 "Junior" steel burner, wicked ready for lighting. Takes ⅝-inch wick. Height over all, 11¾ inches. Wt., 1¾ lbs. ....$ .55
Same style in brass; wt., 1¾ lbs. ....$ .95
Same style, nickel plated.$1.25
Extra globes, white, $ .06; red, $ .20; bull's eye, $ .15.

"Union" Driving Lamp

The Dietz "Union" driving lamp is made with black enamel finish with brass door rim. Has right and left-hand sockets. It is famous the world over as a road illuminant. It complies with all night driving laws of states and cities, and will not jar or blow out. Parts are removable for cleaning, including aluminum reflector. These lamps are widely used by physicians. With optical lens; ruby rear signal. For kerosene. Wicked ready for lighting. Takes ⅜-inch wick, ⅞-inch lens. Height over all 11¼ inches. Wt., 3½ lbs. $3.00

Dietz "Blizzard" Lantern

Dietz No. 2 "Blizzard" cold blast lantern gives a 10-candle power light. It is the most popular "cold blast" lantern on the market and embodies every good technical lantern feature—reinforced tubes, globe lift inside of frame, dome-shaped solderless oil fount, large oil filler, patent safety winglock burner, security standing bail hooked into patented brass eyelets. Made in bright tin. For kerosene; wicked ready for lighting. Size of wick, 1 inch. Height over all, 15 inches. Wt., 2½ lbs..............$ .65
Extra globes, white, $ .08; red, $ .20; bull's eye, $ .15.

Dietz Night Drivers' Friend Lamp

The Night Drivers' Friend is made of cold rolled steel and is designed for use on the side of a buggy top. Reflects 30 candle power light by active test and will light the road 150 feet ahead of the horse. Has a ruby lens which shows plainly from the rear, a plain door lens and is fitted with a removable, nontarnishing, illuminating reflector. The lamp is attached by removing the prop nut from the side brace on the front corner of the buggy top and replacing same permanently with the pointed nut provided. The lamp is seated by slipping the lamp socket over the point of the nut and locking it securely in place with a wire clamp. Can be removed or replaced in a moment. One filling of kerosene burns ten hours. Always specify whether right or left-hand is wanted. Has ⅜-inch wick and weighs 3½ lbs. $3.00

Special "Blizzard" Lantern

The Dietz Special No. 2 "Blizzard" lantern give a 10-candle power light. It is an extra good lantern, with reinforced tubes, globe lift inside of frame, dome-shaped solderless oil fount, extra large, 40-hour burning capacity. Has large oil filler, patent safety wing-lock burner, security standing bail hooked into patented brass eyelets. Made in bright tin only, with wick ready for lighting. Burns kerosene. Size of wick 1 inch. Height over all 15 inches. Wt., 3 lbs. ....$ .85
Extra globes, white, $ .08; red, $ .20; bull's eye, $ .15.

"Blizzard" Dash Lamp

The Dietz No. 2 "Blizzard" cold blast dash lamp gives a superior light and is adaptable to use as a hand lantern or wall lamp. It has a corrugated reflector and bull's eye lens, a solderless fount with safety oil well and all the latest "Blizzard" lantern improvements. It is made in black japan finish. For kerosene, wicked ready for lighting. Has 2½-inch bull's eye lens, 1-inch wick. Height over all 14¾ inches.
Wt., 3½ lbs. $1.00
Extra globes, each.......... $ .20

Conductors' Lanterns

No. 3. Dietz conductors' lanterns are handsome in appearance and substantially constructed. They can be fitted with half colored engraved globes suitably inscribed. Bayonet catch oil pot. For signal oil. Wicked ready for lighting. Nickel-plated. Height over all 8½ inches.
Wt., 2 lbs. $4.50
Extra globes, white, $ .50; half green, $1.50.

Dietz No. 6 Railroad Lantern

This lantern is the best and most convenient lantern using signal oil made. Furnished with the patented reinforced Sangerster spring oil pot and No. 6 lead globe made especially for this lantern. Fount holds sufficient oil to burn 15 hours. Bright tin finish, full height, 10"; 1" wick; wt., 2½ lbs. .... $ .75

"Acme" Inspectors' Lamp

Dietz's improved hot blast inspectors' lamp is in use on all the prominent railway systems of the United States. It is handy and compact, gives a strong reflected light on the work, and the new rigid handle is comfortable and insures the light being thrown at the proper angle, thus preventing the flame from smoking and cracking the globe. This is the only inspector's lamp made with square tubes. Made in bright tin only. For kerosene. Has ⅝-inch wick and patented No. 1 "Acme" burner. Height over all 15½ inches.
Wt., 2½ lbs....... $1.50

Extra globes, white, $ .06; bull's eye......... $ .15

Dietz Improved Vulcan Railroad Lantern

This improved Vulcan is made with round wire guards and skeleton base. The upright guard wires are securely locked to the lower band by metallic strip, making it the strongest lantern of its kind on the market. The Vulcan is equipped with the new patented wing lock burner which fits into slip collar and rests on fiber washer permanently secured to the fount. A short turn of the wrists securely locks the burner to same. The oil fount is held securely to the frame by a patented automatic retaining spring which permits the fount being removed with one hand. The fount is provided with a special well which prevents the oil sloshing and has capacity for 24 hours. The finish is bright tin. 1" wick with outside wick raiser. Full height 10". Wt., 2½ lbs......................... $ .75
Extra globes, white........................ $ .10

Ratchet Lantern Burners

The Dietz No. 1 Special ratchet, long shaft, is a well made signal oil burner, and will accurately fit the screw collars of the lanterns to which it is adapted. It has ⅝-inch wick and No. 1 screw hoop. Made for "Standard," "Steel Clad" and "Vulcan" R. R. lanterns, Nos. 3 and 8 and 39 conductors' lanterns. Wt., 2 oz.......... $ .10
No. 1. Extra special ratchet burner with long shaft. No. 1 extra screw hoop (1-inch wick), for "Steel Clad" and "Vulcan" railroad lanterns and "Steel Clad" rear signal lamp. Wt., 2 oz.... $ .10

Patented Lantern Burners

No. 1. "Blizzard" Dietz patented tinned steel burners for kerosene lanterns. The excellent burning qualities of Dietz lanterns is due largely to the superiority of the Dietz burners employed. This burner has slotted cone and ⅝-inch wick. Used on No. 1 "Blizzard" lanterns, No. 1 "Blizzard" mill lanterns, and No. 15 side lamps. Wt., 2 oz.. $ .10

No. 2 "Blizzard" burner has safety wing lock cone and 1-inch wick. Used on No. 2 "Blizzard" lanterns, No. 2 "Blizzard" mill lanterns, Special No. 2 "Blizzard" lanterns, No. 2 "Blizzard" dash lamps, No. 25 side lamps, and No. 30 Beacon Lights." Wt., 2 oz....................... $ .10

Selected Lantern Globes

Best quality No. 2 Tubular globes, ground level on top and bottom. Weight about 1 lb.
White .... $ .10   Red .... $ .20

DIETZ LANTERNS

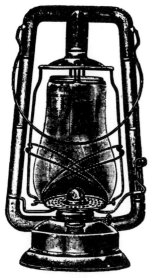

Dietz Monarch O Tubular

Dietz Monarch, O Tubular

Complete with No. 411 Hot Blast Burner, No. 1 wick (⅝-inch) and No. 0 Tubular Globe. Fount capacity, 30 hours. Packed 1 dozen; weight 30 pounds.

Price, per dozen............$16.80

Little Wizard (Cold Blast)

Complete with No. 201 Burner, ⅝-inch Wick, Little Wizard Globe. Fount capacity, 30 hours.

Packed 1 dozen; weight, 24 pounds.

Price, per dozen............$18.50

Little Wizard (Cold Blast)

No. 2 De Lite (Cold Blast)

No. 2 De Lite (Cold Blast)

Complete with No. 262 Burner, 1-inch Wick, No. 100 Short Cold Blast Globe. Fount capacity, 45 hours.

Packed ½ doz.; weight 40 pounds per doz.

Price, per dozen............$26.00

No. 2 Blizzard (Cold Blast)

Complete with No. 262 Burner, 1-inch Wick, No. 2 Cold Blast Globe. Fount capacity, 45 hours.

Packed ½ doz.; weight 40 pounds per doz.

Price, per dozen............$26.00

No. 2 Blizzard (Cold Blast)

Dietz Steel Clad No. 39

No. 39—Dietz Empire, steel clad, spider bottom, outside ratchet, No. 1 extra lard oil burner and No. 2 Wick.

Per dozen $31.00

RAILROAD
Dietz New Vesta

Complete with No. 500 Burner, ½-inch Cosmos Wick and Vesta Globe; lighted and regulated from the outside; made on the tubular principal. For all railroad service.

New Vesta Railroad, for coal oil.

Per dozen $40.00

LANTERNS

Dietz Monarch
Hot Blast

Bright tin; patent reinforced tubes; double seamed solderless dome-shaped oil fount; large oil filler; patent safety wing-lock burner; positive-locking globe lift; Dietz "Fitzall" globe; patent brass eyelets; Security standing bail.

Per Dozen

No. OM—Height over all 13½ inches, ⅝ inch wick; 4 candle power; fount capacity 18 hours; weight per dozen 38 lbs.....................$.....

One dozen in a case

Dietz Royal
Hot Blast

Bright tin; patent reinforced tubes; double seamed solderless oil founts; large oil filler; patent wing-lock burner; positive locking globe lift; Dietz "Fitzall" globe; patent brass eyelets; security standing bail.

Per Dozen

No. 2R—Weight over all 13½ inches; 1 inch wick; 5 candle power; fount capacity 20 hours; weight per dozen 40 lbs.....................$.....

One dozen in a case

Dietz Blizzard
Cold Blast

Bright tin; patent reinforced tubes; double seamed solderless dome-shaped oil fount; large oil filler; patent globe lift on inside of frame; patent safety, wing lock rising cone burner; patent locking Dietz Blizzard globe; Security standing bail; patent brass eyelets.

Per Dozen

No. 2B—Height over all 14¾ inches; 1 inch wick; 10 candle power; fount capacity 20 hours; weight per dozen 52 lbs.....................$.....

Half dozen in a case

Dietz Junior
Cold Blast

All brass; patent reinforced tubes; double seamed dome-shaped solderless oil fount; patent brass eyelets; safety wing lock burner; large oil filler; patent globe lift; Dietz Junior globe.

Per Dozen

No. JCB—Height over all 12 inches; ⅝ inch wick; 6 candle power; fount capacity 13 hours; weight per dozen 32 lbs......$.....

One dozen in a case

LANTERNS

Dietz Little Wizard
Cold Blast

Bright tin; patent reinforced tubes; double seamed solderless, dome-shaped oil fount; large oil filler; patent glove lift on inside of frame; patent safety wing lock rising cone burner, patent lock nob little wizard globe; Dietz security standing bail; patent brass eyelets.

Per Dozen

No. LW—Height over all 11½ inches; ⅝ inch wick; 6 candle power; fount capacity 18 hours; weight per dozen 30 lbs..........................$.....

One dozen in a case

Dietz Regular Fount
D-Lite
Cold Blast

Bright tin; patent reinforced tubes; double seamed solderless dome-shaped oil fount; large oil filler; patent safety, wing lock rising cone burner; patent locking, Dietz D-Lite short globe; Dietz security standing bail; patent brass eyelets.

Per Dozen

No. 2D—Height over all 13¼ inches; 1 inch wick; 10 candle power; fount capacity 20 hours; weight per dozen 50 lbs.....................$.....

Half dozen in a case

Dietz Large Fount
D-Lite
Cold Blast

Bright tin fount and top; patent reinforced tubes; extra large double seamed, solderless, dome-shaped oil fount; large oil filler; patent safety, wing lock rising cone burner, tinned steel; patent globe lift on inside of frame; patent locking D-Lite (Lock-Nob) Dietz short glove; Dietz security standing bail; patent brass eyelets.

Per Dozen

No. 2DLF—Height over all 13¾ inches; 1 inch wick; 10 candle power; fount capacity 40 hours; weight per dozen 48 lbs.........$.....

Half dozen in a case

Dietz Standard Railroad

Substantial stamped base and top; double guard; globe is removed through frame by turning back the hinged top; No. 1 patented wing lock ratchet burner attached to fount by patented locking lugs; base fastens to frame by patented positive locking device operated by a twist of the hand; fount has safety oil well; heat resisting globe for signal oil.

Per Dozen

No. 39—Height over all 10 inches; 1 inch wick; 2 candle power; fount capacity 24 hours; weight per dozen 45 lbs..........$.....

One dozen in a case

LANTERNS
HOT BLAST

Air is drawn over the top of the globe into the tubes and from thence down to the burner. It comes in contact with the heat of the globe and is therefore hot when entering the tubes.

LEADER
HOT BLAST

Bright tin. No. 1 steel burner. ⅝-inch wick. No. 0 globe. Steel filler. Upward lever. Bottom lift.

With Stained Ruby Globe

No.	Height	Burns	Ship. wt. doz.	Per doz.
140R	14 in.	18 hrs.	25 lbs.	$19.20

With Clear Globe

140	14 in.	18 hrs.	25 lbs.	$18.00

One dozen in a case.

DIETZ MONARCH

Bright tin. Positive locking lift. No. 411 steel burner. ⅝-inch wick. 4 C. P. light. Dome fount with brass oil filler. Uses our Nos. 0, R0, or R10 globes.

No.	Height	Burns	Ship. wt. doz.	Per doz.
1M	13½ in.	20 hrs.	38 lbs.	$19.50

O. K.

Bright tin. Tip-out globe mechanism. ⅝-inch wick. 4 C. P. light. Flat fount. Brass filler. Uses our 0, R10 and R0 globes.

	Height	Burns	Ship. wt. doz.	Per doz.
O. K.	13 in.	20 hrs.	37 lbs.	$21.50

All above, one dozen in a case.

DIETZ ACME INSPECTOR
HOT BLAST

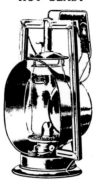

Bright tinned steel, with hood. Inset fount bottoms. Filler cap and screw. Wide band tin handle with flat top. 5-inch silvered reflector. No. 0 globe. No. 551 steel burner, carrying a ⅝-inch wick. Used by car inspectors and others who need concentrated white light. 20 C. P. light.

Reinforced square tubes. Braced frame and hoods.

No.	Height	Burns	Ship. wt. doz.	Per doz.
1A	15½ in.	20 hrs.	36 lbs.	$72.00

One-half dozen in a case.

DIETZ BUCKEYE DASH

Black enamel finish. Corrugated bright tin reflector. Positive locking lift. No. 411 cone burner. 10 C. P. light. ⅝-inch wick. Dome fount. Brass oil filler. Uses No. 0 globe.

No.	Height	Burns	Ship. wt. doz.	Per doz.
1BD	13¼ in.	20 hrs.	52 lbs.	$32.00

One-half dozen in a case.

DIETZ NEW EUREKA SIDE OR DRIVING

Black enameled steel. 3⅛-inch door lens. 2¼-inch rear ruby lens. 1½-inch side green lens. Side attachment. No. 561 steel burner. ⅝-inch wick. Used as automobile parking lamp. Saves battery current.

Specify Right or Left Hand

	Height	Burns	Ship. wt. doz.	Per doz.
E. D.	7¼ in.	10 hrs.	19 lbs.	$38.00

One dozen in a case.

LANTERNS

Dietz Junior Wagon Cold Blast

Black enameled tin; combination holder for round or flat bracket; bright tin reflector; magnifying bullseye lens on plate; ruby rear lens danger signal to the rear; standing bail, brass eyelets; tinned steel safety wing lock rising cone burner; reinforced tubes; large oil filler; double seamed solderless dome shaped oil fount with safety oil well; patented globe lift on inside of frame; Dietz Junior globe.

Per Dozen

No. JW—Height over all 12 inches; fount $\frac{5}{8}$ inch wick; 10 candle power; capacity 13 hours; size of ruby rear lens $2\frac{1}{4}$ inches; size of bullseye $2\frac{1}{4}$ inches; weight per dozen 58 lbs........................$.....

DIETZ LANTERNS.

3R4052— Dietz's No. 2 De-lite Cold Blast Lanterns. Cannot be spoken of too highly. Made on the cold blast principle and **will not blow out in any wind.** Bottom lift; globe removable without disturbing the guard. No. 2 burner (1 inch wick); packed ½ dozen in crate, 24 lbs. Per doz..................... **13.00**

R4052—In less than case lots. Dozen 13.25

3R4054—Dietz No. 2 De-lite. With extra large fount; burns 40 hours; wt. 26 lbs. to ½ doz. case Doz........... **14.25**

R4054—In less than case lots. Dozen 14.50

3 R 4055— **Dietz Special No. 2 Blizzard.** The King of cold blast lanterns; give a light of 10 c. p. They are fitted with Dietz No. 2 blizzard burners, 1 inch wick and blizzard globe; will burn 40 hours. Finish bright tin. **Strongest and best lantern made;** ½ doz. in case; wt. 30 lbs. Per dozen.. **13.00**

R 4055 — In less than case lots. Doz................... 13.25

3R4059—Dietz No. 2 Blizzard; as above; large fount; burns 40 hours. ½ doz. in box. Doz..................... **14.25**

R4059—As above. Less than case lots. Doz..................... **14.50**

DIETZ BOY SPORT LANTERNS FORMERLY CALLED "BOY SCOUT."

3R4057 — Sport Lantern. Not a toy but a real practical lantern that will burn steadily in wind or storm; built like all Dietz lanterns, strong; light in weight; 10 hour fount capacity; 7¾ in. high; ⅝ in. wick; 1 candle power light; retinned finish; 1 doz. in case. Doz.......... **6.00**

½ doz. lots. Doz... 6.25

R4050—Extra White Globes. Dozen .... .80

WONDER JUNIOR LANTERNS.

Burns Oil

R4058 — Junior Lantern; made of heavy bright tin plate; top and bottom screw-on; can be taken apart to clean; white globe; burns thirty-six hours one filling; size 3 1/3 diameter; 6 ¾ ins. high; loop bail; 4 ins. high; 1 doz. in box. Per doz. **2.00**

DIETZ
"LITTLE WIZARD" LANTERN

(COLD BLAST)

FITTED WITH DIETZ PATENT "LOC-NOB" SHORT GLOBE. THE GLOBE THAT ACTU-ALLY LOCKS FAST . IMPOSSIBLE TO DROP OUT WHEN GLOBE HOLDER IS TIPPED BACK.

No. 1 BURNER   5/8 INCH WICK   6 C. P.

The DIETZ "LITTLE WIZARD" is the smallest Short Globe Lantern made. It is but 11 1/2" inches high and with the same size wick gives 50% more light than the ordinary No. 0 Lantern.

The Short Globe is half the height of a No. 0 Globe. It is convenient to clean and there is practically no breakage from overheating. The Fount is double-seamed and guaranteed oil-tight. It holds sufficient oil to burn 18 hours.

The No. 1 Burner (5/8 inch wick) is of the Dietz patent winglock pattern. The rising cone enables the user to trim and light the wick with ease.

DIETZ
"No. 2 Large Fount Wizard" Lantern

FITTED WITH DIETZ PATENT "LOC-NOB" SHORT GLOBE. THE GLOBE THAT ACTU-ALLY LOCKS FAST IMPOSSIBLE TO DROP OUT WHEN LANTERN IS OPENED.

NO. 2 BURNER   1 INCH WICK   10 C. P.

EXTRA LARGE FOUNT HOLDS 32 OUNCES OF OIL. WILL BURN 40 HOURS WITH MAXIMUM POWER.

Otherwise same construction as Dietz "No. 2 Wizard" Lantern including winglock burner with rising cone, standing bail etc. Furnished in bright tin and tin with brass fount and top.

DIETZ
"ROADSTER" WAGON LANTERN

WITH 21/4 INCH RUBY REAR LENS

No. 1 BURNER   5/8 INCH WICK   10 C. P.

(COLD BLAST)

The DIETZ "ROADSTER" WAGON LANTERN will meet the requirements of State and City laws regulating night lights on moving vehicles. It has the clip-spring holder in addition to the combination socket taking a round or flat bracket. Gives a powerful light ahead and at the same time shows a danger signal to the rear.

The "ROADSTER" has a bright, corrugated reflector and magnifying bullseye lens fixed in permanent focus.

BLACK ENAMEL FINISH.

WHY "DIETZ" LANTERNS EXCEL

The Original DIETZ TUBULAR LANTERN was placed on the market in 1868, over forty-eight years ago.

DIETZ STANDARD LANTERNS are made from the very best material, IXAA tin, and the best tinned wire. Quality has distinguished "DIETZ" Lanterns for three generations.

DIETZ STANDARD LANTERNS are the only make having a patent brass eyelet in the tubes. The bail cannot tear out. A kink in the eyelet holds the bail upright.

DIETZ PATENT SAFETY WINGLOCK STEEL BURNERS will outlast any brass burner. They are guaranteed superior in every way, give a better light, *and are locked securely to the air chamber.*

DIETZ GLOBES are all selected, evenly ground on top and bottom, are free from streaks and blemishes, and fit the Lanterns perfectly.

DIETZ GLOBES are solid color, no dipped Globes are put into DIETZ Lanterns.

DIETZ was first to equip Lanterns with "Loc-Nob" Globes to prevent dropping out when cleaning, trimming or lighting.

DIETZ CROSS-WIRE GUARDS were an identifying feature of DIETZ Lanterns for years. Imitators are now using this guard in order to have their Lanterns appear like "DIETZ".

DIETZ was first to make Lanterns with square tubes; the first as well to make them with round stamped tubes.

DIETZ was first to make "ribbed" tubes adding great strength and rigidity to the frame.

DIETZ was first to furnish a dome-shaped fount on a Tublular Lantern. It not only adds symmetry to the Lantern, but strength as well.

DIETZ was first to double-seam the bottom of Lantern Oil Founts, *thus forming a solderless oil-tight fount.*

DIETZ was first to equip Lanterns with an extra large filler cap and collar.

DIETZ STANDARD LANTERNS are provided with a patent Side Lever for raising and lowering the globes. This lever *securely locks the globe in place.*

DIETZ LANTERNS have the greatest efficiency of candle power. *From actual photometric test,* they give a light of from 4 to 10 candle power.

ALL GENUINE DIETZ LANTERNS are plainly stamped (DIETZ)

The name "DIETZ" has been a Lantern Guarantee for three generations.

BRIEF LANTERN HISTORY

The Original
First tubular lantern produced in 1868 to burn newly refined fuel made from Pennsylvania crude. Our newest designed lamp appropriately carries this name.

The Junior
One of our first cold blast lanterns introduced in 1880. Designed to utilize cold air in the combustion chamber to improve light output.

The Little Wizard
A streamlined cold blast lantern with a fuel capacity for extended usage. Introduced in the 1930's. Excellent camping lamp.

The Air Pilot
A modified cold blast D-Lite lantern utilizing a wide wick for brighter light, and large mouthed globe for easy cleaning. Also excellent for camping.

For years to come, your Dietz Hurricane Lantern will provide you with the warmth of a charming atmosphere while providing you simple illumination.

DIETZ HURRICAN LANTERNS AND REPLACEMENT PARTS

210-01060 LITTLE WIZARD (BLUE)
208-51003 CLEAR GLOBE
288-00010 WICK

210-08060 AIR PILOT (Blue)
208-54003 CLEAR GLOBE
288-00020 WICK

210-10060 MONARCH (Blue)
208-52003 CLEAR GLOBE
288-00010 WICK

210-21060 JUNIOR (Blue)
208-57003 CLEAR GLOBE
288-00010 WICK

210-51060 COMET (Blue)
208-48003 CLEAR GLOBE
288-00130 WICK

210-76060 ORIGINAL (Blue)
208-56003 CLEAR GLOBE
288-00060 WICK

210-80060 BLIZZARD (Blue)
208-52003 CLEAR GLOBE
288-00020 WICK

210-90060 D-LITE (Blue)
208-50003 CLEAR GLOBE
288-00020 WICK

Other Colors and Solid Brass available in some models.

Dietz Lanterns Since 1840
In 1840 the Dietz Lantern Company was formed. From whale oil lamps, the company grew to embrace kerosene, acetylene and other lamp fuels as they developed. Today, the recommended fuels are common lamp oil, clear or colored, citronella oil to repel bugs outdoors or kerosene. From Erie Canal packet boat lamps, Jenny Lind concert chandeliers, clipper ship running lights, Civil War locomotive lanterns, and horse-drawn trolley lights to kerosene auto lamps, acetylene head and tail lights, a Dietz product has always been lighting the way. We hope you enjoy your Dietz Lantern.

Safety Operation & Maintenance
Proper care means more enjoyment. Your authentic Dietz Hurricane Lantern is exceedingly safe to use and incorporates a wind resistance feature. There is no compressed fuel, or tanks to contend with. To use your Dietz Lantern properly, follow these simple instructions before lighting.

Trim Wick Properly
First press down on the globe lever to raise the globe (see page 4 for parts description). Although your lantern was shipped from our factory with wicks properly trimmed, time and transportation may have damaged your wick, or given it a "fuzzy" appearance. If damage is evident, cut straight across with sharp scissors, making the top flat and squaring the edges. This will cause your wick to burn more evenly, giving you longer burning time, and better light. The same holds true for a charred wick after steady use (see figure 1).

Fig. 1

Next with your wick adjusting ratchet, (see figure 4), adjust the wick height to no more than 1/16 inch above the flame plate. You are now ready to fill your lantern.

Fill Your Lantern Properly
Fill reservoir only to bottom of filler cap. Do not tip lantern back to get more fuel in, as this will cause your lantern to leak. You are now ready to light your lantern.

Use Only Approved Fuel
The recommended fuels are COMMON LAMP OIL, clear or colored, CITRONELLA OIL, to repel bugs out doors, or KEROSENE.
Warning: Under no circumstances should you use Coleman Lantern and Stove fuel, or any type of gasoline. These fuels are extremely flammable, and if used in a wick lantern, could cause an explosion.

Lighting Your Dietz Lantern
With the globe in the raised position, light the wick. Return the globe to the lowered position. Within a few minutes your lantern will warm to operating temperature. This will result in a higher flame. Using your wick adjusting ratchet (globe remains in lowered position) you can increase or decrease flame height for best illumination. If wick starts to burn and smoke, then you have the wick too high.

Wick & Globe Replacement
Grasp the bail and lift up on the chimney ring as illustrated in Fig. 2. Tilt the globe away from the filler cap to horizontal position. Open cross guard as depicted in Fig. 3. Gently lift globe through cross guard and out of the lantern. Grip adjusting ratchet and push either right or left as shown in Fig. 4. This removes the air plate and burner assembly. Remove old wick. Install new wick. Reverse procedure to re-assemble lantern components.

Fig. 2

Fig. 3

Fig. 4

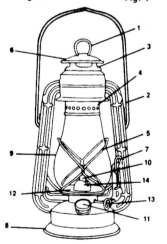

Description
1. Chimney Ring
2. Bail
3. Chimney
4. Globe Holder
5. Cross Guard
6. Chimney Cap
7. Globe Lever
8. Fount
9. Globe
10. Wick
11. Fuel Cap
12. Flame Plate
13. Wick Adjusting Ratchet
14. Air Plate and Burner Assembly

SECTION II

ADLAKE LANTERNS

Manufactured by the Adams and Westlake Company. These pages are originally from catalog and bulletins from the years 1907 to 1922.

If you would like an exact date we recommend "Lanterns That Lit Our World".

The Adams & Westlake Company

New York   **CHICAGO**   **Philadelphia**

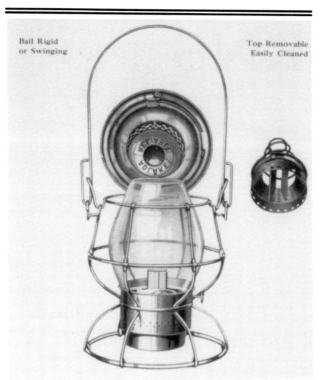

The Adlake Reliable Lantern with Removable Top
Globe Holder and Rigid Bail Lock

*Bail Rigid
or Swinging*

*Top Removable
Easily Cleaned*

The Adams & Westlake Company

New York   Chicago   *Philadelphia*

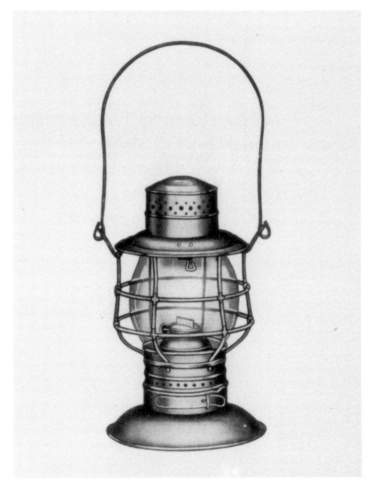

No. 39 Double Guard Wire Railroad Lantern

Fitted with lard oil ratchet burner to take No. 1, ⅝-inch, or No. 2,
1-inch wick.

Adlake Acetylene Gas Conductors' Lantern

Made of Brass and Heavily Nickle Plated.

Takes the Pullman Conductor Globe.

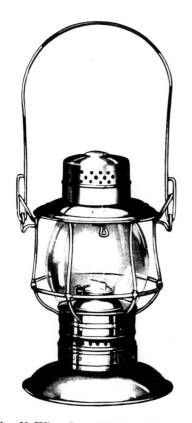

No. 39 Wire Guard Railroad Lantern

Fitted with inside wick raiser, lard oil ratchet burner to take No. 1, ⅜-inch, or No. 2, 1-inch wick.

Note the Baffle Plates in the Top Globe Holder, which prevent draughts from putting out the flame.

Adlake Perfected Ventilation

Removable Top Globe Holder

Rigid Bail Lock

The Adams & Westlake Company

New York   Chicago   *Philadelphia*

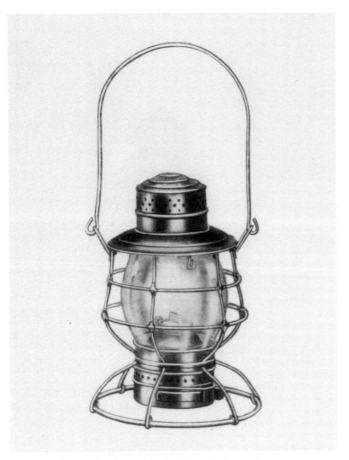

No. 11 Double Guard Wire Railroad Lantern

Fitted with lard oil ratchet burner to take No. 1, ⅝-inch, or No. 2, 1-inch wick.

The Adams & Westlake Company

New York   Chicago   *Philadelphia*

Conductors' Lanterns
Made of Brass and Heavily Silver or Nickel Plated

"The Queen"
Closed Bottom

"The Queen"
Open Bottom

"The Pullman"

The Adams & Westlake Company

New York   Chicago   *Philadelphia*

No. 7 Steamboat Lantern

Takes No. 7 Lake and River globe.
Fitted with lard oil ratchet burner to take No. 1, ⅝-inch or No. 2, 1-inch wick.

The Adams & Westlake Company

New York   Chicago   *Philadelphia*

Tri-Color Lamp

For track walkers, taking the place of three lanterns. It has a revolving cylinder inside carrying red and green signals; operated from without by the bail, and fixed in position by means of a flat spring at the back, with stop catch.

Policeman's or Watchman's Dark Lamp

Made of brass or heavy tin

The Adams & Westlake Company

New York   Chicago   *Philadelphia*

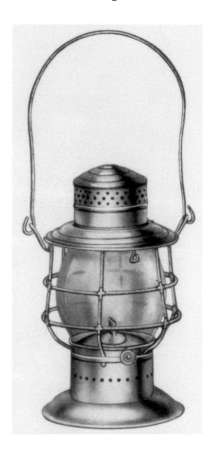

No. 39 Double Guard Wire Railroad Lantern

With Outside Wick Raiser

Fitted with lard oil ratchet burner to take No. 1, 5⁄8-inch, or
No. 2, 1-inch wick.

The Adams & Westlake Company

New York   Chicago   *Philadelphia*

Outside Wick Raiser Lanterns

Method of Adjusting Flame

No complicated mechanism.
Burner shaft extends to outside of lantern.
Flame adjustable without removing oil-fount or globe.
Oil-founts cannot be lost, as *solid bottom* prevents their
dropping out.

34

No. 90 Rigid Wood Bail Switchman's Lantern

This Wooden Bail allows a firmer grip on the lantern for yard service.

Adlake Perfected Ventilation

Removable Top Globe Holder

Equipped with an easily detachable bent wood rigid bail, makes control of signal easy.

Standard No. 39 globe, made to withstand hard service.

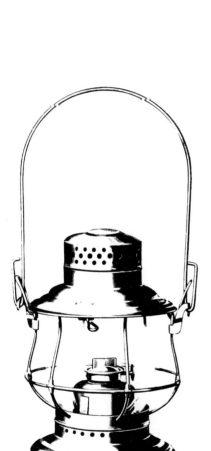

**No. 91 Combination Swinging and Rigid Bail
Switchman's Lantern**

Our new design of top makes it easier to keep the lantern bright.

Adlake Perfected Ventilation

Removable Top Globe Holder

Rigid Bail Lock

Standard No. 39 Globe

No. 199 Drawbridge Lamp.
Adlake Non-Sweating Balanced Draught Ventilation.

Made of heavy steel throughout.

Fitted with one 8-inch diameter 360-degree white pressed Fresnel lens, two 8 3/8-inch ruby, and two 8 3/8-inch green roundels.

This is the lamp referred to in paragraph six of the United States Specifications, and the last lamp referred to in paragraph one of the Canadian Specifications.

The Adams & Westlake Company

New York   Chicago   *Philadelphia*

No. 40 Steamboat Lantern

Takes 6 x 6-inch Government globe.
Fitted with lard oil ratchet burner to take No. 1, 5/8-inch or No. 2, 1-inch wick.

No. 196 Channel, Sheer Boom, or Coast Lamp.
Adlake Non-Sweating Balanced Draught Ventilation.

Made of heavy steel throughout.

Fitted with 8-inch diameter 360-degree pressed Fresnel lens.

This lamp can be fitted with either white, green or ruby Fresnel lens.

With green Fresnel it is the lamp referred to in paragraph five of the United States Specifications.

With ruby Fresnel it is the lamp referred to in paragraph ten of the United States Specifications.

No. 197 Pier or Abutment Lamp.
Adlake Non-Sweating Balanced Draught Ventilation.

Made of heavy steel throughout.

Fitted with 8-inch diameter 180-degree pressed Fresnel lens.

Can be fitted with either white, green or ruby Fresnel lens.

With ruby Fresnel this is the lamp referred to in paragraph seven of the United States Specifications.

With white Fresnel this is the first lamp referred to in paragraph one of the Canadian Specifications, and the last lamp referred to in paragraph two of the Canadian Specifications.

Adlake Encased Oil Pot

¶ Another feature of this Adlake Reliable Lantern is the outside wick-raiser. In addition to saving time, it does away with smoky globes, and the danger of the light going out in the course of adjustment. The outside wick-raiser permits the operator to turn the wick a little higher for lighting and then to readjust the size of the flame after the lantern is warm and the oil is feeding more rapidly than at first.

¶ And finally, to show the ease with which this lantern may be lighted we reproduce the above photograph showing the manner in which, nine times out of ten, a railroad lantern is lighted. The operator holds the lantern in his left arm, unsnaps the cover with the fingers of his right hand, inserts the fingers of his left hand under the lower edge of the globe, and through this crack inserts the lighted match with his right hand.

¶ Any manner of lighting a lantern involving the use of a drop bottom style of oil pot, involves on the part of the operator the use of three hands, — one to hold the lantern, one to hold the match, and one to hold the oil pot.

1st Movement
    Opening cover

2nd Movement
    Removing globe

3rd Movement
    Lifting lantern to
    remove oil pot

4th Movement
    Removing oil pot

5th Movement
    Replacing lantern

6th Movement
    Removing burner

7th Movement
    Filling oil pot

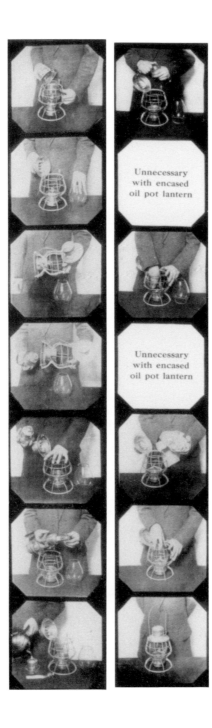

8th Movement
    Replacing burner

9th Movement
    Lifting lantern to
    replace oil pot

10th Movement
    Replacing oil pot

11th Movement
    Replacing lantern

12th Movement
    Cleaning globe

13th Movement
    Replacing globe

14th Movement
    Closing cover

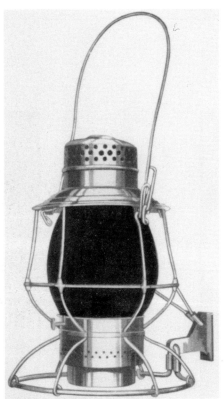

**No. 11 Wire Guard Electric Railway Tail Lantern
With Red Globe**

Fitted with outside wick raiser, lard oil ratchet burner to take
No. 1, ⅝-inch, or No. 2, 1-inch wick.

The Encased Oil Pot is
the "ounce of preven-
tion" kind of equipment.

Adlake Perfected Ventilation
Removable Top Globe Holder
Encased Oil Pot
Outside Wick Raiser
Rigid Bail Lock

**No. 11 Adams Steel Guard Electric Railway Tail Lantern
With Red Globe**

Fitted with outside wick raiser, lard oil ratchet burner to take
No. 1, ⅝-inch, or No. 2, 1-inch wick.

The Rigid and
Swinging Bail
Lock makes
one Lantern
as convenient
as two.

Adlake Perfected Ventilation
Removable Top Globe Holder
Rigid Bail Lock

(Front and Side View shown at right)

8-Inch 90 Degree Ruby Fresnel Platform Tail Lamp No. 33
(Missouri Pacific Standard)

The No. 33 Platform Tail Lamp has been designed and developed in response to a demand for a lamp that will give a safe divergence of signal on a sharp curve. The standard bracket tail lamps have but slight divergence. Such a light could not be seen on a sharp curve until trains were dangerously close together. This lamp obviates such dangers completely. Its signal divergence is sufficient to warn a following train on the sharpest curves.

The efficiency of any lamp depends on its ventilation. The only ventilation which keeps the lenses clear, and renders the lamp safe from draughts at rest and in motion, is the Adlake Non-Sweating Balanced Draught.

We have combined wide angle signaling power and perfect ventilation in a well made, japanned steel lamp that cannot fail to give satisfaction.

Front View

The Adams & Westlake Company

New York   Chicago   *Philadelphia*

**Adlake
Non·Sweating
Balanced Draught**

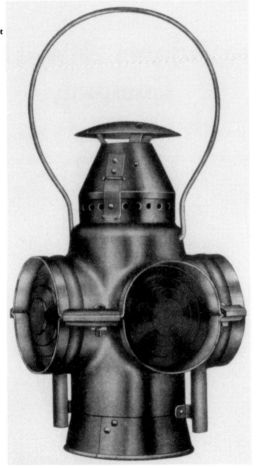

Side View

No. 63 Pressed Steel Switch Lamp, arranged for Fork
Non-sweating Ventilation

Heavy steel throughout.

Oil-pot enters lamp at bottom.

Fitted with 4½-inch and 4⅛-inch or 5⅜-inch lenses.

Equipped with one-day or long-time burner, as desired.

Body pressed from two plates of heavy steel; clamped and bolted together.

The Adams & Westlake Company

New York   *Chicago*   *Philadelphia*

No. 73 Switch Lamp

Made of galvanized iron.
Sliding door, drawn oil-pot and cast base.
Equipped with 5-inch lenses, long-time or one-day burner, as desired.

The Adams & Westlake Company

New York   **CHICAGO**   **Philadelphia**

Adlake Non-Sweating Ventilation

Maximum Signalling Efficiency

No. 83 Round Body Steel Marker or Tail Lamp

Sliding door. Equipped with 1, 2, 3 or 4 lenses. Colors as desired. Heavy steel throughout. Lenses 5¾ inches unless otherwise specified. Adjustable bracket permits lamp to be easily revolved with one hand.

Adlake Non-Sweating Balanced Draught Ventilation insures clear lenses and maximum efficiency.

The Adams & Westlake Company

New York　　　　　*Chicago*　　　　　*Philadelphia*

Adlake
Non-Sweating
Balanced Draught

No. 161 Round Body, Steel Tail Lamp

With bracket socket.
Heavy steel throughout.
Otherwise, same as No. 208, page 96.

The Adams & Westlake Company

New York　　　　　*Chicago*　　　　　*Philadelphia*

Adlake
Non-Sweating
Balanced Draught

No. 168 Round Body, Steel Marker or Tail Lamp
Non-sweating Ventilation

Heavy steel throughout.
Equipped with 1, 2, 3 or 4 lenses, of colors and sizes desired.

The Adams & Westlake Company

New York   *Chicago*   *Philadelphia*

Adlake
Non-Sweating
Balanced Draught

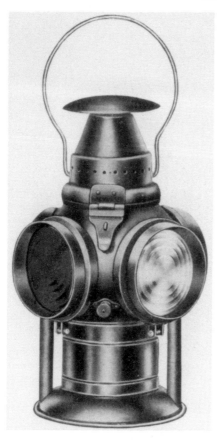

No. 169 Pressed Steel Switch Lamp,
arranged for Fork

Outside wick raiser.
Heavy steel throughout.
All parts readily accessible for cleaning.
Equipped with one-day or long-time burner, as desired.
Hinged top. Spiral springs in fork tubes relieve jar on lamp.
Fitted with 4-inch, 4 1/8-inch, 4 1/2-inch, 5-inch, 5 3/8-inch lenses.

The Adams & Westlake Company

New York   *Chicago*   *Philadelphia*

Adlake
Non-Sweating
Balanced Draught

No. 169 1/2 Round Body, Steel Tail Lamp

With discs for day signals.
Equipped with fork tubes or spring socket base.
(See pages 57 and 58 for lamp description.)

The Adams & Westlake Company

New York   *Chicago*   *Philadelphia*

Adlake
Non-Sweating
Balanced Draught

The "S" style bracket, doing away as it does, with "right hand" and "left hand" lamps is a great advantage to railroads as it reduces by half the number of these lamps that must be carried in stock.

The lever system of changing the color discs which we use for No. 187 and No. 187½ has proved itself most satisfactory for this service. The lever system is simple in its operation and will not become disarranged or get out of order.

No. 206 Round Body Steel Switch Lamp
Non-sweating Ventilation

Sliding door.
Outside wick raiser.
Heavy steel throughout.
Spring socket base relieves jar on lamp.
Fitted with two 5-inch and two 41/2-inch lenses.
Equipped with one-day or long-time burner as desired.

No. 187 Lamp
with Style "F" Bracket.

No. 187½ Lamp
with Style "R" Bracket.

Adlake Non-Sweating Balanced Draught Ventilation.

The Adams & Westlake Company

New York   *Chicago*   *Philadelphia*

Adlake
Non-Sweating
Balanced Draught

No. 208 Round Body, Steel Tail Lamp

Non-sweating Ventilation

Sliding door.
With dash hangers.
Heavy steel throughout.
One 4 or 53/8-inch ruby lens; other size lens if desired.

The Adams & Westlake Company

New York   *Chicago*   *Philadelphia*

Adlake
Non-Sweating
Balanced Draught

No. 209 Round Body, Steel Tail Lamp

Non-sweating Ventilation

With rigid bracket.
Otherwise, same as No. 208.

The Adams & Westlake Company

New York   CHICAGO   Philadelphia

The No. 251 Round Body Steel Marker or Tail Lamp is the same as our standard No. 83 Round Body Steel Marker or Tail Lamp, except that it has Adlake Square-Top Ventilation and Wind-Proof Door.

The distinctive merits of Adlake Square-Top Ventilation and Wind-Proof Door are emphasized in detail in Bulletin B-31.

Equipped with one, two, three or four lenses, as desired.

The No. 270 Straight Body Steel Marker or Tail Lamp with ADLAKE Square-Top Ventilation and Wind-Proof Door.

The No. 270 is the same as the No. 251, illustrated on page 4, except that it is made with a straight body of one continuous piece of metal, instead of with a bell bottom.

No. 219 Round Body, Steel Tail Lamp

Adlake Non-Sweating Balanced Draught Ventilation

The Adams & Westlake Company

New York   Chicago   *Philadelphia*

Adlake
Non-Sweating
Balanced Draught

No. 3 Pressed Steel Semaphore Lamp

Non-sweating Ventilation

41/8-inch lenses.
Heavy steel throughout.
Oil fount enters lamp at bottom.
One-day or long-time burner, as desired.
For interlocking, automatic block, or train order signals.

The Adams & Westlake Company

New York   Chicago   *Philadelphia*

No. 6 Square Body Semaphore Lamp

Side door for removing oil-pot.
Upper draught system of ventilation.
Fitted with one 53/8-inch white lens and one 2-inch white
bull's-eye.

The Adams & Westlake Company

New York   Chicago   *Philadelphia*

No. 7 Square Body Semaphore Lamp

Side door for removing oil-pot.
Lower draught system of ventilation.
Fitted with one 5³/₈-inch white lens and one 2-inch white bull's-eye.

The Adams & Westlake Company

New York   Chicago   *Philadelphia*

Adlake
Non-Sweating
Balanced Draught

No. 9 Interior of Semaphore Lamp

Showing long-time burning fount, with one-way metallic parabolic reflector.

The Adams & Westlake Company

New York   Chicago   *Philadelphia*

Adlake
Non-Sweating
Balanced Draught

No. 10 Round Body, Steel Train Order Signal Lamp

Heavy steel throughout.
One-day or long-time burner as desired.
Fitted with two white lenses of any desired size, otherwise same as No. 9 Semaphore Lamp shown on previous page.

The Adams & Westlake Company

New York   Chicago   *Philadelphia*

No. 81 Bottom Draught, Round Body Semaphore Lamp

Tin or steel.
One 5 3/8-inch white lens and one 2-inch bull's-eye.

The Adams & Westlake Company

New York   Chicago   *Philadelphia*

**No. 107 Old Type Harrington
Semaphore Signal Lamp**

The Adams & Westlake Company

New York   Chicago   *Philadelphia*

Adlake
Non-Sweating
Balanced Draught

**No. 140 Round Body,
Steel Semaphore Lamp**

Non-sweating Ventilation

Heavy steel throughout.
Same as No. 9 Semaphore Lamp (page 67), expect that it
has special socket for banjo signals.

The Adams & Westlake Company

New York   Chicago   *Philadelphia*

Adlake
Non-Sweating
Balanced Draught

No. 158 Round Body, Steel Semaphore Lamp

Non-sweating Ventilation

Heavy steel throughout.
For Harrington signal.
Otherwise same as No. 9 Semaphore Lamp (see page 67).
One-day or long-time burner, as desired.

The Adams & Westlake Company

New York   CHICAGO   Philadelphia

No. 173 Distinctive Permissive Signal Lamp

Adlake Non-Sweating Balanced Draught Ventilation

FRONT VIEW   BACK VIEW

No. 187, Red, Green and White Signals

No. 187 Adlake Automatic Engine Classification Lamp is made of heavy steel throughout. It is fitted with 5-inch or 5¾-inch white lenses and ruby and green color discs, permitting its use as a Classification or

No. 187 closed.

Tender Marker Lamp. This lamp is shown fitted with style "S" bracket, and can be used on either side of the locomotive.

Fitted with Adlake Non-Sweating Balanced Draught Ventilation.

No. 187 open.

No. 180 SEMAPHORE LAMP

This lamp more than satisfies the requirement of the Railway Signal Association, as will be seen by reference to pages 2 and 3 of this Bulletin. The perfect ventilation of this lamp, upon which depends its efficiency, is the result of years of development and test, under actual conditions of service.

Among the advantages offered by this lamp are:

Rigid Serviceable Structure.
    Full Brilliant Flame.
        Convenient adjustment of Flame from outside.
           Long time Burner.
               Perfect Ventilation.
                   Ability to withstand any weather.
                     Wind Proof Door.
                         Maximum Signaling Efficiency.
                       Unfogged Lenses.

No. 187½, Green and White Signals Only

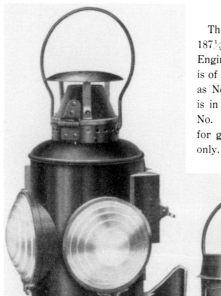

The construction of No. 187½ Adlake Automatic Engine Classification Lamp is of the same high character as No. 187. The difference is in the colors of signals, No. 187½ being equipped for green and white signals only.

No. 187½ closed.

These lamps are standard on many of the largest Railroad Systems. This lamp is shown fitted with style "S" bracket, and can be used on either side of the locomotive.

Fitted with Adlake Non-Sweating Balanced Draught Ventilation.

No. 187½ open.

The Adams & Westlake Company

New York   Chicago   *Philadelphia*

Adlake
Non-Sweating
Balanced Draught

No. 204 Pressed Steel Semaphore Lamp

Non-sweating Ventilation

Hinged top.
Heavy steel throughout.
One-day or long-time burner, as desired.
For interlocking, automatic block, or train order signals.
Same body design as our No. 169 (page 57) Pressed Steel Switch Lamp.

The Adams & Westlake Company

New York Chicago *Philadelphia*

The Adams & Westlake Company

New York Chicago *Philadelphia*

Adlake
Non-Sweating
Balanced Draught

Adlake
Non-Sweating
Balanced Draught

No. 9 Round Body Steel Semaphore Lamp

Non-sweating Ventilation

Sliding long door.
Heavy steel throughout.
With or without backlight.
Fitted with lens of any desired size.
One-day or long-time burner as desired.
May be equipped with metallic or prism glass reflector.

No. 207 Round Body, Steel Convertible Semaphore or Train Order Signal Lamp

Non-sweating Ventilation

One-day or long-time burner.
Lenses and discs interchangeable.
Two lens-openings of any size desired.
Sliding door. Heavy steel throughout.
May be fitted with Prism glass or metallic reflector if desired.
For Automatic Block Signals: Steel blank replaces backlight.
For Train Order Signals: Equipped with two white lenses.
For Semaphore Signals: Equipped with white lens, and steel disc in which is fitted backlight.

The Adams & Westlake Company

New York   Chicago   *Philadelphia*

No. 82 Bottom Draught, Round Body Train Order Lamp

Tin or steel.
Two 5 3/8-inch white lenses.

The Adams & Westlake Company

New York   Chicago   *Philadelphia*

Adlake
Non-Sweating
Balanced Draught

No. 130 Round Body, Steel Tail or Classification Lamp

Non-sweating Ventilation

With dash hanger.
Heavy steel throughout.
Bracket substituted for hanger, if desired.
Equipped with one 5 3/8-inch white lens, hinged to permit
the insertion of colored glass behind lens to change signal.

The Adams & Westlake Company

New York   Chicago   *Philadelphia*

Adlake
Non-Sweating
Balanced Draught

No. 15 Platform Tail Lamp

Non-sweating Ventilation

Has 8-inch ruby lens.
For rear platform of coach or caboose.
A plain white glass on each side, 4 1/2-inch diameter serves
to light platform of car.

The Adams & Westlake Company

New York   Chicago   *Philadelphia*

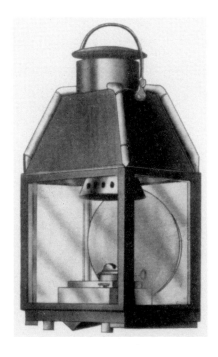

Tubular Station Platform Lamp

The flame in this lamp will endure rough winds.
No. 1 (No. 1 burner), 5/8-inch wick, 6-inch silvered glass reflector.
No. 2 (No. 2 burner), 1-inch wick, 7-inch silvered glass reflector.
No. 3 (No. 3 burner), 1 1/2-inch wick, 12-inch silvered glass reflector.
It will burn 24 hours without refilling, and is adapted for railway
stations, barns, packing-houses, mills, etc.

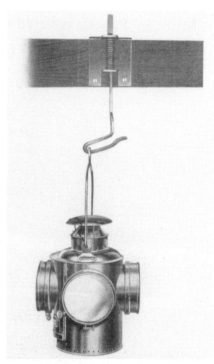

Showing gate in closed position

ADLAKE CROSSING GATE LAMP No. 52
WITH HANGER No. 1

One of the problems in connection with Crossing Gate Lamps has been that when the gate is dropped, it comes to a sudden stop when the support meets the street, and this causes the oil in the wick to be jarred down, and if the shock is sufficient, the flame will be extinguished.

The Adams & Westlake Company

New York   **CHICAGO**   **Philadelphia**

No. 1120
HIGHWAY CROSSING GATE LAMP
(One Light)
Pennsylvania System Standard

Approved for regular equipment at R. R. crossings requiring <u>dependable</u> danger signals.

(For specifications see opposite side this bulletin)

The Adams & Westlake Company

New York   Chicago   *Philadelphia*

Adlake
Non-Sweating
Balanced Draught

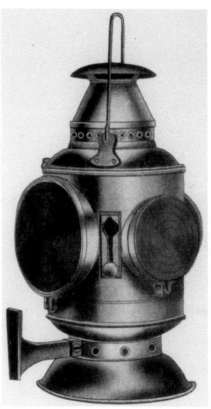

No. 78 Steel Marker or Tail Lamp

Non-sweating Ventilation

Hinged top.
Colors as desired.
Heavy steel throughout.
Equipped with 1, 2, 3 or 4 lenses.
Lenses 5 3/8-inches unless otherwise specified.

The Adams & Westlake Company

New York   Chicago   *Philadelphia*

Adlake
Non-Sweating
Balanced Draught

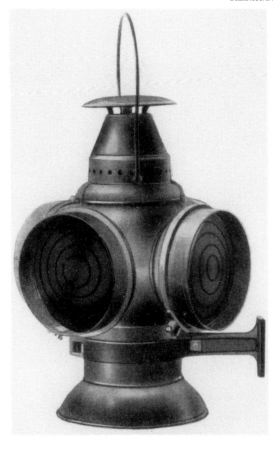

No. 203 Pressed Steel Marker or Tail Lamp

Non-sweating Ventilation

Hinged top.
Heavy steel throughout.
All parts readily accessible for cleaning.
Lenses 5 3/8-inches unless otherwise specified.
Equipped with 1, 2, 3 or 4 lenses; colors as desired.

The Adams & Westlake Company

New York   Chicago   *Philadelphia*

Adlake
Non-Sweating
Balanced Draught

No. 60 Tail Lamp

Non-sweating Ventilation

For elevated train.
Heavy steel throughout.
Equipped with one 5 3/8-inch ruby lens.
Side door for removing oil-pot and lighting lamp.
Back of lamp is angled to suit shape of platform rail, over
which fits the bracket attached to back of lamp.

The Adams & Westlake Company

New York   Chicago   *Philadelphia*

Adlake
Non-Sweating
Balanced Draught

No. 193 Square Body, Steel Tail Lamp

Non-sweating Ventilation

Heavy steel throughout.
Special bracket attachment.
Equipped with one 5 3/8-inch ruby lens.

The Adams & Westlake Company

New York   **CHICAGO**   Philadelphia

The No. 252 is the same as our well known No. 187 Engine Classification Lamp, except that is has Adlake Square-Top Ventilation and Wind-Proof Door.

The distinctive merits of Adlake Square-Top Ventilation and Wind-Proof Door are emphasized in Bulletin B-31.

Equipped with automatic color changing device.

Lamps fitted with standard "R" brackets (as shown) unless otherwise ordered. For other types of brackets see Bulletin B-18.

The No. 252½ Engine Classification Lamp with Adlake Square-Top Ventilation and Wind-Proof Door.

The No. 252½ Engine Classification Lamp is the same as the No. 252, except that it is equipped for green and white signals only.

List of repair parts on pages 2 and 3.

The Adams & Westlake Company

New York Chicago *Philadelphia*

The Adams & Westlake Company

New York Chicago *Philadelphia*

Adlake
Non-Sweating
Balanced Draught

No. 190 Round Body, Steel Revolving Caboose Cupola Lamp

Non-sweating Ventilation

Heavy steel throughout.
One 6-inch ruby lens; one 6-inch green lens.
With automatic steel slide for blinding red lens; operated from inside of caboose.

No. 190 Round Body, Steel Revolving Caboose Cupola Lamp

Non-sweating Ventilation

Heavy steel throughout.
One 6-inch ruby lens; one 6-inch green lens.
With automatic steel slide for blinding red lens; operated from inside of caboose.

The Adams & Westlake Company

New York Chicago *Philadelphia*

Adlake
Non-Sweating
Balanced Draught

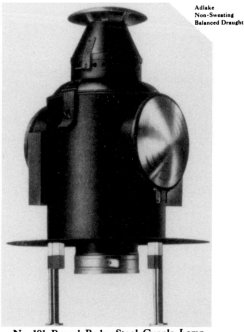

Adlake
Non-Sweating
Balanced Draught

No. 191 Round Body, Steel Cupola Lamp

Non-sweating Ventilation

Heavy steel throughout.
Signals changed from interior of caboose and are operated by vertical sliding movements. Interlocking device automatically locks one color disc above lens while other is in position back of lens, displaying desired signal.
Equipped for red, green, or white signals.
Fitted with two 5-inch white lenses.

No. 191 Round Body, Steel Cupola Lamp

Non-sweating Ventilation

Heavy steel throughout.
Signals changed from interior of caboose and are operated by vertical sliding movements. Interlocking devise automatically locks one color disc above lens while other is in position back of lens, displaying desired signal.
Equipped for red, green, or white signals.
Fitted with two 5-inch white lenses.

The Adams & Westlake Company

New York   **CHICAGO**   Philadelphia

The No. 275 Pressed-Steel Switch Lamp with spring-socket base and 28 ounce oil fount is the same as our standard No. 175 Switch Lamp, except that it has Adlake Square-Top Ventilation.

The distinctive merits of Adlake Square-Top Ventilation and Wind-Proof Door are explained in Bulletin B-31.

Equipped with one-day or long-time burner as desired. Has a hinged top and outside wick raiser. The spiral springs in the base relieve the jar on the lamp.

The Adams & Westlake Company

New York   **CHICAGO**   Philadelphia

View from street.

Adlake
Crossing Watchman's
or
Crossing Gate Lantern
No. 319
With Hanger No. 1

View from street

Under normal weather conditions the danger signal is plainly discernible 3000 feet from the track. The coiled spring hanger eliminates the possibility of light failure through sudden jar such as would be caused by the hurried lowering of the crossing gate.

Adlake long-time or one day burners can be furnished as desired.

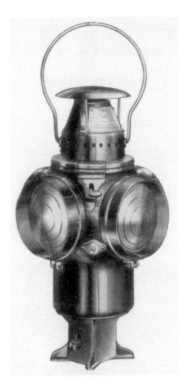

**Adlake Standard No. 175 Switch Lamp
with 28-ounce oil fount**

Adlake Standard No. 175 Switch Lamp with either an
Adlake long time or one day burner, equipped with 28-oz.
oil fount. This lamp is well constructed of heavy pressed
steel, with malleable iron base, and can be furnished with
or without spring socket. It has the Adlake Balanced
Draught Non-sweating Ventilation which insures unfogged
lenses and maximum signalling efficiency. This large oil
fount has sufficient capacity to render more than two visits
a week of the lamp tender unnecessary. Except for the oil
fount, all parts of this lamp are interchangeable with the
corresponding parts of the Standard No. 169 Switch Lamp.

No. 175½ Switch Lamp with Day Signal Targets

Our No. 175½ Switch Lamp is identical with No. 175
except that it is equipped with day signal targets, and a
long enough wick raiser shaft to extend beyond the targets.
It is equipped with a 28 ounce oil fount, holding sufficient
oil to make more than two visits a week of the lamp
tender unnecessary. The targets can be furnished in any
color required.

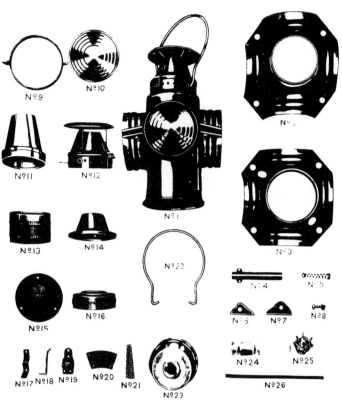

Parts No. 63 Switch Lamp

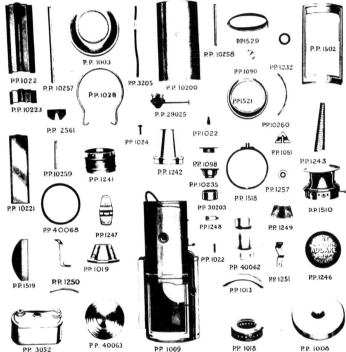

Parts of No. 180 Semaphore Lamp

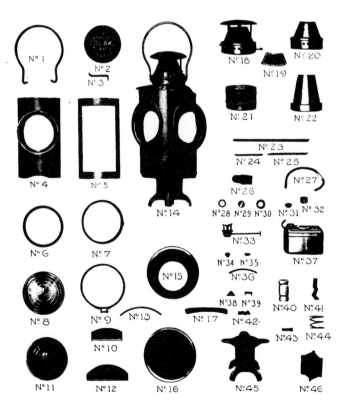

Parts of No. 216 Switch Lamp

WILLIAM PORTER'S & SONS

The "Porter" R. R. Hand Lantern.

Spring bottom.

Made of tin. Height 10 inches. dia meter base 6 inches. Base fastened by patent process, cannot become detached, as in other makes. Flange at bottom of upright guards greatly strenghtens the lantern. We guarantee this to be the strongest hand R. R. lantern made.

White,	-	10.00 Doz.
Ruby,	-	18.00 "
Green or Blue,	-	15.00 "

The "Pet" Conductor Lantern.

Same as No. 297, except has bayonet catch. Height, 9½ inches. Diameter of base, 5 inches. A great favorite.

Brass,	- -	54.00 Doz.
Nickel Plated,	- -	66.00 "
Heavy "	- -	78.00 "

Add 2.00 Each for Colored Globes.

297

The "Porter" Conductor Lantern.

Made of brass, also nickel or silver-plated. Burns signal oil, with ratchet burner. Height, (not including handle), 10 inches; diameter of base, 6 inches. Lamp springs in at bottom, and has drip cup to catch any overflow of oil. The handsomest lantern made.

Brass,	- -	60.00 Doz.
Nickel Plated,	-	84.00 "

Add 2.00 Each for ½ Colored Globes.

The "Porter" R. R. Hand Lantern.

Bayonet Catch.

Same as No. 294, except has side spring or bayonet catch.

White,	-	10.00 Doz.
Ruby,	-	19.00 "
Green or Blue,	-	16.00 :

The "Porter" 89, R. R. Hand Lantern.

Bayonet Catch.

Same as No. 295, except has no flange, and takes No. 89 globe.

White,	-	10.00 Doz.
Ruby,	- -	18.00 "
Green or Blue,		15.00 "

426

Extra Strong Lantern for Kerosene. $10.00 Dozen.

427

Extra Strong Lantern for Lard or Sperm Oil. Tin, $10 00 Dozen. Brass, $24.00 Dozen.

THE "BROADWAY" TAIL LAMP.

Made of tin, painted. Two 4½ in. Fresnel Lenses. Burns kerosene or other oil. A cheap strong lamp. - 4.25 Each.

The "Manhattan" Tail Lamp.

Made of tin, painted. One 5-inch red Semaphore Lense. Burns any oil as ordered. Made Rights and Lefts, fasten on rear of platform rail. The elevated R R. standard.
5.00 Each.

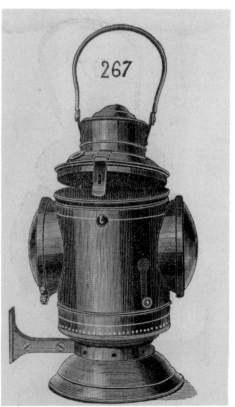

The "Universal" Tail Lamp.

Made of heavy tin, painted. Two 5 inch Semaphore Lenses. (Fitted with colored glass slides). Burns kerosene or other oil as ordered. A companion lamp to No. 277. A perfect end train signal. Made with socket (as shown) to fasten on hood or iron loop to fasten on side of car.

424
Common Hand
Lantern. $6.75 Doz.

The "Penn" Tail Lamp.

Made of heavy tin, painted. Four 4½ in. Fresnel Lenses with two covers. (Fitted with colored glass slides.) Burns kerosene or other oil. The P. R. R. Standard.
5.00 Each.

300

Locomotive Guage Lamp.

Made of brass. Glasses are adjustable.
Extreme height, 8 inches. A very serviceable lamp. In general use.
$3.00 Doz.

301

**Bull's Eye Locomotive Gauge
Lamp.**

Made of brass. One or two bull's eyes,
3 inches. Extreme height, 8 inches.
1 Bull's Eye,   -   35.00 Doz
2   "   "   -   - 38.00 "

The "Cyclone" Engine Signal.

Made of heavy tin, painted.   Three 5
inch Semaphore lenses, showing colors, as
ordered.   Has all latest improvements.
Burns kerosene or other oil as ordered.
The Best Engine Signal Made.   Either
fastening same as No 267.

Locomotive Head Light.

Made with 12, 14, 16, 18 20 and 23 inch reflectors. Case
painted plain black.   These lamps are made in the best manner
possible, and are not excelled by any head light manufactured.

12 & 14 inch, each	-	49.50
16 " "	-	64.50
18 " "	-	72.00
20 " "	-	79.50
23 " "	-	87 00
23 in. Standard, (cheap)	-	57.00

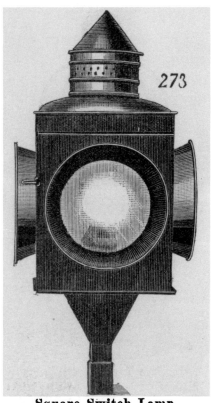

The "Georgia" Engine Signal.

Made of brass or tin, painted. Three 3½ inch plain bulls eye lenses with colored glass slides. Burns signal oil. A very strong, neat lamp. Has loop and socket at back to fasten.

Brass, - 6.00 Each.
Tin, - - 4.00 "

Square Switch Lamp.

Made of heavy tin, painted. Four 5-in. Lenses, plain or Semaphore, with colored glass as ordered. Burns kerosene or other oil. Has iron socket to fit rod. An old and much used pattern.

10.00 Each.

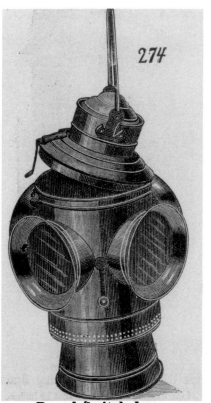

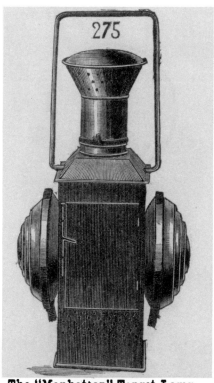

Round Switch Lamp.

Made of heavy tin, painted. Two each, red and green, 4 inch Semaphore Lenses. Burns kerosene or other oil, as ordered. Has iron socket to fit on rod.

5.00 Each.

The "Manhattan" Target Lamp.

Made of heavy tin, painted. Height 17 inches (not including handle). Two 6-inch Semaphore lenses with colored slides. Burns kerosene or other oil as ordered. "Manhattan" Elevated Railway standard.

6.00 Each.

200

Cylinder-shaped Signal Lantern.

Made of tin or brass: Heavy glass, Large oil pot for kerosene (⅜ wick) or other oils as ordered. Height over all 16 in. A favorite pattern.

Tin, - - 22.00 Doz.
Brass, - - 36.00 "

425
Common Square
Lantern. $5.25 Doz.

Tri-Color Signal, or Track Master's Lamp.

Made of tin, painted. Beveled glass front. Height over all 14½ inches. Revolving cylinder, shows red, green, or white light at will of operator. Burns kerosene or other oil as ordered. An invaluable lamp for track walkers.

246
Bull's Eye Lantern.
Made of brass or tin. 2¼ in. bull's eye.
Tin Jap., $7.00 Doz.
Brass, 30.00 "

434
Brass. 10.50 Dozen.

436
Pocket Lamp.
$6.75 Dozen.

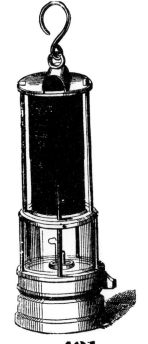

431
"Humphrey Davy"
Safety Lantern. $78.00 Dozen

430
Brass Lantern.
Height 10 in. $9.00 Dozen.

433
All Styles of Tubular
Lanterns. $7.12 Dozen

432
$18.00 Dozen.

428
Heavy Square Lanterns for
Warehouses, &c. $12.00 Dozen.

429
Japanned Fancy Lantern.
Height 9 in. $14.00 Dozen.

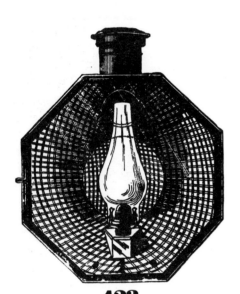

423
Corrugated Tin Reflector Lantern.
$3.25 Each.

437
Police Lanterns.
2¾ in. Bulls Jap. $6.00 dz.
3   "   "   "   7.50 "
2¾ " Brass.   30.00 "
3   "   "   36.00 "

438
Flat Police Lantern.
2 in. Bulls, Jap. $6.00 dz.

440
Dashboard Lamp.
$15.00 Dozen.

441
Dashboard Lamp.
$21.00 Dozen.

Side Lights—Port and Starboard.

Made of Brass. ⅝ inch wick. Chimney burner for Mineral-Sperm. or kerosene oil. Size of glass, 6x16 in. Height (not including handle 16 in. Matches Nos. 207 and 213.

33.00 Pair.

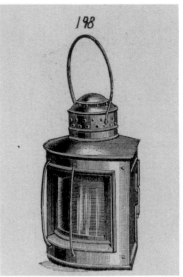

Side Lights—Port and Starboard.

Made of galvanized iron or brass. Burns kerosene, ⅝ in. wick. Plain bent glass 3¼x5¼ in. Height (not including handle) 9¼ in.

Brass, fancy, - 12.00 Pair.
Galvanized - 5.25 "

Side Lights—Port and Starboard.

Made of tin. Painted. Burns kerosene. ⅝ in. wick. Plain bent glass, 3¼x5¼ in. Height (not including handle) 10 in. The "Hard Pan" Side Light.

3.75 Pair.

Side Lights—Port and Starboard.

Made of galvanized iron or brass. Burns kerosene. ⅝ in. wick. Plain bent glass, 4¼x6¼. Height over all, 13 in.

This pattern also made "NEW REGULATION" size. (See No. 195.)

Galvan., - 5.63 Pair.
Brass, - 11.25 "

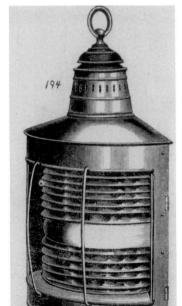

Side Lights—Port and Starboard.

Made of galvanized iron. 1 in. wick. Burns kerosene or heavy oil if so ordered. Size of glass 7x11 in. Height over all 20 in. English Channel size. Matches Nos. 206 and 214.

24.00 Pair.

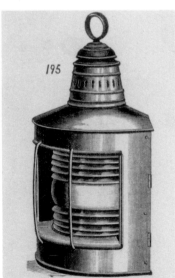

Side Lights—Port and Starboard.

Made of galvan. iron or Brass. ¾ in. wick. Burns kerosene or heavy oil if so ordered. Size of glass 6x6 in. Height over all 17 in. "NEW REGULATION" size, Matches Nos. 205 and 215.

This size made also with plain bent glass, same pattern as No. 197.

Galvan., - - - 12.00 Pair.
Brass, - - - 24.00 "
Galvan., plain glass, - 8.00 "
Brass, " " - 16.00 "

Side Lights—Port and Starboard.

Made of Brass. Chimney or no chimney burner. For kerosene (1 in. wick) or other oils as ordered. Size of glass, 7x11 in. Height (not including handle) 19 in. English Channel size. Matches Nos. 212 and 206 or 208.

45.00 Pair.

Club Boat Lanterns.

Made of brass. Burns kerosene. Height over all 11½ in. Shows Port and Starboard at sides. White light ahead. Used extensivley by Rowing Clubs.

7.50 Each.

Side Lights—Port and Starboard.

Made of galvan. iron. ⅝ in. wick. Burns kerosene. Size of glass 4½x6½. Height over all 15 in. Matches Nos. 204 and 216.

Galv'd, 9.00 Pair.

Steamboat half round Binnacle Lamp.

Made of brass. Size of front 6x7 in. Smaller size 5x5½ in. Other patterns made to order.
Large, $4.00 each.
Small, 3.50 "

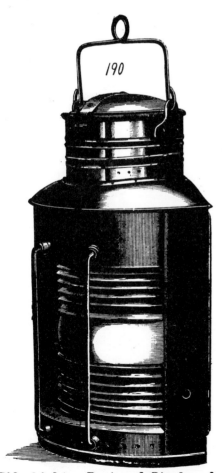

Side Lights—Port and Starboard.

Made of Brass, 1 in. wick. Chimney burner for Mineral-Sperm, or Kerosene oil Size of glass 9x10 in. Height (not including handle) 20 in For largest class of vessels. Matches Nos. 208 and 211.

55.00 Pair.

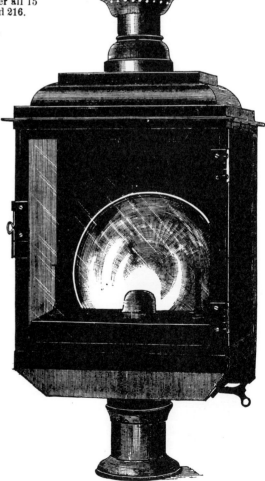

The "ELLIS," adopted by the U. S. Navy.

Made of heavy brass, nickled. Front glass, 11x12; side, 7x12 Burns lard oil, without chimney, giving very brilliant light.

$34.50 each.

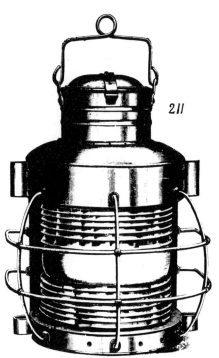

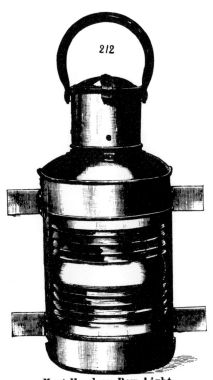

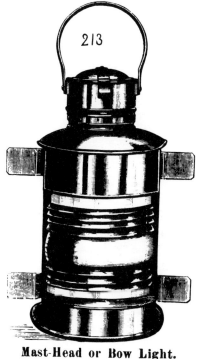

Mast-Head or Bow Light.

Made of brass (1 in. wick). Chimney burner for Mineral-Sperm or kerosene oil. Size of glass, 9x22 in, Height, (not including handle) 20 in. Matches with No. 190, Side Light.

35.00 Each.

Mast-Head or Bow Light.

Made of brass. Chimney or no chimney burner. For kerosene (1 in. wick) or other oils as so ordered. Size of glass, 7x12 in. Height (not including handle) 19 in. English Channel size. Matches No. 191.

20.00 Each.

Mast-Head or Bow Light.

Made of brass. Chimney burner for Mineral-Sperm or kerosene oil (⅝ in. wick). Size of glass, 6x8 in. Height, (not including handle) 16 in. Matches Nos. 192 and 207.

15.00 Each.

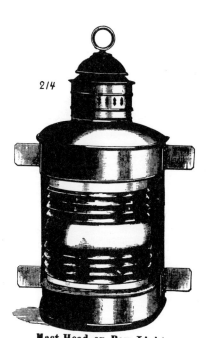

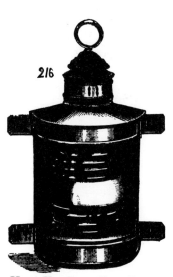

Mast-Head or Bow Light.

Made of galvanized iron. Burns kerosene (1 in. wick). Size of glass, 7x12 in. Extreme height 21 in. Matches Nos. 194 and 206.

12.00 Each.

Mast-Head or Bow Light.

Made of galvanized iron or brass. Burns kerosene (¾ in. wick.) Size of glass, 6x6 in. Extreme height, 18 in. Known as "Regulation" size. Matches Nos. 195 or 196, and 205.

Galv'd iron,	5.25 Each.
Brass,	10.50 "

Mast-Head or Bow Light.

Made of galvanized iron or brass. Burns kerosene (¾ in. wick). Size of glass, 5x6. Extreme height, 14 in. Matches Nos. 197, 198 and 204.

Galv'd Iron,	4.50 Each.
Brass,	8.00 "

Anchor Light.

Made of galvan. iron or tin. Japanned; for kerosene (⅜ in wick) or oil. Globes 8 in. diameter. Height over all, 19 in. Suitable where a cheap 8 in. Anchor Light is wanted.

Square Smack Anchor Light.

Made of Tin ; burns kerosene 2 sizes ; large, 9x13; small, 8x10 in. glass. A great favorite with smack owners.

Anchor Light.

Made of galvan. iron or brass; burns kerosene (⅜ in. wick). Fresnel globe 4 in. diameter. Height over all, 15 in.

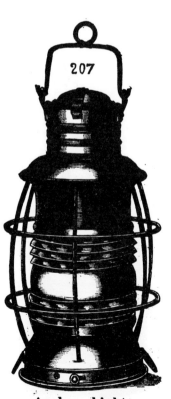

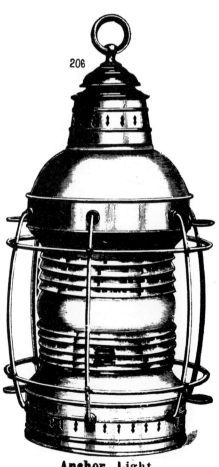

Anchor Light.

Made of galvanized iron or brass. Burns kerosene (⅜ in wick). Fresnel globe, 6 in diameter. Height over all, 17 in. This size more extensively used than any other.

Anchor Light.

Made of brass. Chimney burner for Mineral Sperm or kerosene oil (⅜ in. wick). Fresnel globe, 6 in. diameter. Height (not including handle,) 15 in. Very strong and durable. Shows brilliant light. Matches Nos. 192 and 213.

Anchor Light.

Made of galvanized iron or brass. Burns kerosene (1 in. wick). Fresnel globe, 8 in. diameter. Height over all, 24 in. This light is large enough to cover shipping regulations of any country,

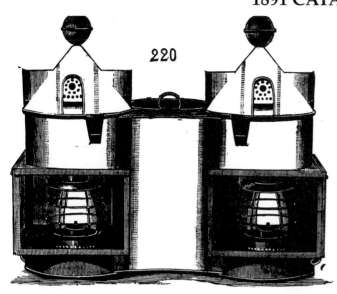

220

STERN OR POLE BOX LIGHTS – For Steamboats. Made to order, of heavy tin, painted. In ordering give diameter of flag pole, at top of upper rail. 15.00 to 35.00 each.

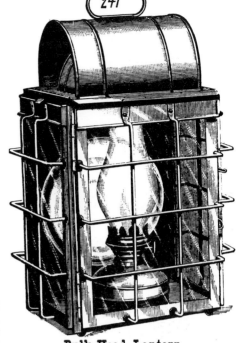

241

Made of galvanized iron, heavy riveted guards. Burns Mineral-Sperm or kerosene oil (1 in. wick) size of glass, 8 x .2 and 6 x 12, double-thick. Nickel plated reflector. For main deck, hold, & c., or where an extra strong, heavy guarded Lantern is needed. 7.50 ea.

Bulk-Head Lantern.

208

Anchor Light.

Made of brass or zinc. Chimney burner for Mineral-Sperm or kerosene oil. Fresnel globe 8 in. diameter. Height (not including handle), 18 in. Matches Nos. 190 and 211. The very best Anchor light produced. A regular "Lighthouse."
Brass . . . . 20.00 ea
Zinc . . . . 15.00 "

209

Anchor Light.

Made of galvanized iron, zinc or brass. Burns kerosene (1 inch wick) or heavy oil, if so ordered. Glass 10 inch in diameter. Height over all, 20 in. Galv'd or Zinc – 5.00 ea. Brass – 7.50 ea.

276

Pole Target Lamp.

Made of brass or zinc. Extreme height 18 inches, Glass 6 inches diameter. Burns kerosene or other oil, as ordered. An old and well known pattern.
Brass –9.00 ea. Zinc–6.00 "
Add 2.55 for Blue, Red or Green

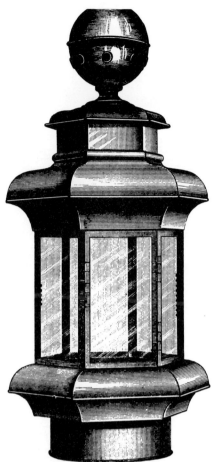

No. 468—Ferry-Boat Pilot House Lantern.

We make these lanterns to order of any desired size and shape, of brass, copper or tin, gilded or not gilded.

Lamps for above either for gas or oil as required, which cost additional.

Price on application.

Bulk-Head Lantern.

No. 2 size. Made of heavy tin (painted) or brass. No guards; otherwise same as No. 241. No. 1 size, glass, 5x10 and 6x10 in. wick, ⅞ in. No. 0 size, glass 4x8 and 5x8 in. wick ⅝ in.

Tin, No. 2 size,	-	5.00	Each.
" " 1 "	-	4 25	"
" " 0 "	-	3.75	"
Brass,	2 "	-	9.00	"
"	1 "	-	8.00	"

Ferry Boat or " Double-ender " Signal.

Made of galvanized iron, copper or brass. 2 sizes- No. 1, two 7 x 11; No. 2 – 6 x 6 glass. To burn gas or oil as ordered. Height No. 1 – 26 in., No. 2 – 20 in. When bow of boat is reversed the colors in lamp are changed by simply sliding screen.

Galv'd Large size	. . . .	50.00 pair
" Small "	. . . .	38.00 "
Copper, Large	. . . .	63.00 "
" Small	. . . .	51.00 "

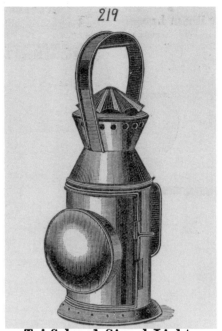

Tri-Colored Signal Light.

Made of brass. 4 in. bull's eye. Burns kerosene or other oil. Extreme height, 14½ in. Shows red, green, white or no light, at the will of operator. A new and invaluable lamp for pilots and others.

Egg-shaped Signal Lantern.

Made of galvanized iron, for kerosene (⅜ wick) or oil. Height over all 18 in. Used extensively on Tow Boats for stern lights.

25.00 Doz.

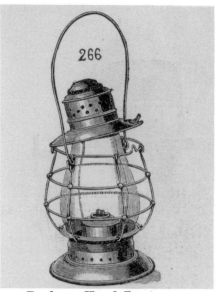

Deck or Hand Lantern.

Made of brass or tin. Burns Kerosene or oil as ordered. Height, (not including candle) 10½ in. No stronger or better lantern produced, and is the U. S. Navy Standard.

Brass, $24.00 dozen.
Tin, 10.00 "
Add $1.25 dozen for Kerosene.

189—Relieving Signal Lamp.

Made of Brass. Same burners, height &c., as No 190. Designed to replace either side or head light in case one become disabled. Shows either red, green or white. A very valuable and useful light.

75.00 Each.

Signal Light.

Red globe; 10 in. diameter. Bail at bottom; otherwise same as No. 209.

"Any vessel not under command, through accident or otherwise must display 3 10-in. red lights, in a vertical line one over the other."

Galv'd Iron or Zinc, - 7.50 Each.
Brass, - - - 10.00 "

Lamp Lighter.

Made of brass. Extreme length, 9¼ inches. Much used on steamships.

$2.75 each.

217

Launch Bow Light.

Made of brass. Burns kerosene (⅝ in. wick). Adjustable socket. Height (not including handle or socket 10½ in. Matches No. 198.

8.00 Each.

218

Row Boat Light.

Made of brass. Height over all 15 in. Can be removed from socket and used as a hand lantern. Will not blow out.

2.00 Each.

255

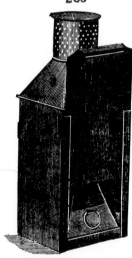

Pilot's Time Light.

Made of Copper. No glass. Body, 4x5 in. Height, 12¼ in. Shows no light in pilot house unless sliding door is raised.

$9.00 each.

435

A Size. $13.50 Dozen.
B Size. $18.00 Dozen.

299

Locomotive Gauge Lamp.

Made of brass. No. 1 with hood (as shown). No. 2 without hood; No. 3 without hood or top; Height of lamp as shown 11 inches. Casting at bottom to screw on rod.

56.00 Doz.

258

Cigar Lighter.

Made of brass. Height 8 in. No glass to be broken, and will not blow out. For steamship smoking room.

$6.00 each.

439

Wagon Lamp, for Candle.
$45.00 Dozen.

PEERLESS No. 2.
COLD BLAST LANTERN.

Made of Charcoal Tin Plate.

Has two piece Stamped Tubes.

Side Lift.

Can be filled or lighted without removing the globe.

Founts are tested for leaks with compressed air.

Gives strong, brilliant light.

Will not blow out in the highest wind.

Bail stays just where you leave it.

Has No. 2 Cold Blast Burner.

1 inch Wick, Cold Blast Globe.

Packed one dozen in a box.

Weight 47 lbs. to dozen.

W. W. HARPER CO., Zanesville, Ohio.

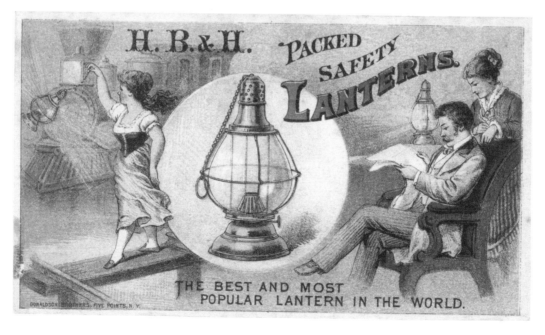

LANTERNS AND DRIVING LAMPS

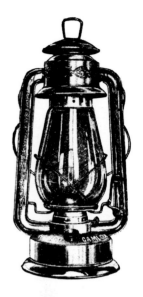

No. 0—HOT BLAST TUBULAR

Side lift, plain globe. Made from heavy gauge I X tin. Height with bail down, 13½ inches. Capacity fount, 1 pint.

Per Dozen......................... $ 6.00
One dozen to case.

No. 0—HOT BLAST DASHBOARD

Side lift, bull eye globe. Made of heavy I X tin. Blue Japanned. Height, bail down, 13½ inches. Capacity fount, 1 pint.

Per Dozen......................... $10.00
One-half dozen to case.

No. 2—COLD BLAST

Side lift, plain globe, No. 2 burner. Capacity oil fount, 1 quart. Made of heavy tin.

No. 240—Tin fount...Per Doz., $12.00
No. 241—Copper fount.Per Doz., 15.00
One-half dozen to case.

COLD BLAST DASHBOARD

Side lift, bull eye globe, No. 2 burner. Made of heavy tin, blue Japanned. Holds one quart of oil.

Per Dozen......................... $15.00
One-half dozen to case.

GEM COLD BLAST DRIVING LANTERN

Black enameled. 2-inch Ruby lens in reflector, showing red rear warning. Height, bail down, 12 inches. Burns 16 hours.

Complete with bracket.

Per Dozen......................... $18.00

DANDY COLD BLAST DRIVING LAMP

Black enameled. 5¾ inch beveled plate lens, silvered reflector, 1¼ inch Ruby lens rear warning. Fitted with dash clamps to attach either side, also spring dash clip and bail. Burns 29 hours.

Per Dozen......................... $48.00

PAULL LANTERNS

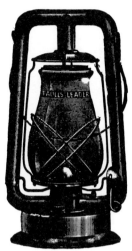

No. 140

No. 140—O Tubular Lantern

Complete with No. 0 Burner, No. 0 Wick (½ inch) and No. 0 Tubular Globe. 16 oz. Fount. Packed ½ or 1 dozen in a case; weight per dozen 26 lbs.

Price, per dozen, packed 1 dozen $13.70

Price, per dozen, packed ½ dozen 14.00

Enameled Red, same price as Plain Tin.

No. 180 Cold Blast Lantern

Complete with No. 2 Cold Blast Burner, 1-inch Wick and No. 2 Cold Blast Globe. 32 oz. Fount. Packed ½ dozen; weight, 32 lbs. per dozen.

Price, per dozen..............$19.90

Enameled Green, same price as Plain Tin.

No. 180—2 Cold Blast

No. 230 Junior Ezy-Lit

Complete with No. 0 Burner, ½ inch Wick and Little Wizard Globe. 16 oz. Fount. Packed 1 dozen; weight per dozen, 30 lbs.

Price, per dozen..............$15.00

Enameled Red, same price as Plain Tin.

No. 250 Ezy-Lit

Same as No. 230 with 32 oz. Fount. Packed ½ dozen to case; weight per dozen, 27 lbs.

Price, per dozen..............$18.00

Enameled Red same price as plain tin.

No. 220 Ezy-Lit—Large Fount Short Cold Blast

Complete with No. 2 Cold Blast Burner, 1 inch Wick and No. 100 Globe. 32 oz. Fount. Packed ½ dozen to case; weight per dozen, 40 lbs.

Price, per dozen..............$19.90

Enameled Green, same price as Plain Tin.

No. 230

No. 220

IF IT'S A HAM'S
YOU CAN DEPEND ON IT

Thirty-six years' experience in the manufacturing of outdoor lanterns and lamps enables us to supply the trade with Tubular Lanterns and Lamps that excel all other makes in burning qualities, strength of construction, style and finish.

We use only the best IX tin and wherever possible the goods are made with locked seams instead of being soldered and therefore there is no chance of their coming apart by becoming unsoldered.

Ham's No. 20 Cold Blast Search Light

We operate the largest and most complete exclusive lantern and lamp factory in the world and we strictly guarantee every lantern and lamp we make to be perfect in every respect or we will gladly replace with perfect goods without any expense to the user.

Insist on Ham's goods—our name is on every Lantern and Lamp we make. Write for complete catalogue showing complete line, it's free. Address "Dept. T."

Office, Factory and Warehouse of The C. T. Ham Mfg. Co. Established 1886
Devoted Exclusively to the Manufacturing of Tubular Lanterns and Lamps.

Lamps.

TIN TUBULAR, SIDE REFLECTOR LAMP.

No. 11.

5 INCH SILVERED GLASS REFLECTOR.

NO. 1 BURNER.   ⅞ INCH WICK.   NO. 0 GLOBE.

No. 11.—Side Reflector Lamp. Plain Finish......Per dozen, $13 50

No. 11.—Side   "   "   Japanned   "......   "   14 50

IMPROVED GLOBE HANGING. SIDE REFLECTOR LAMP.

No. 4.

SILVERED GLASS REFLECTOR.

BOTTOM LIFT.   OUTSIDE WICK REGULATOR.

PATENT WIND BREAK.

No. 4.—Globe Tubular Hanging Lamp, No. 2 Burner
and No. 2 Globe......................Each, $5 00

NEW IMPROVED SQUARE TUBULAR LAMP.

No. 6.

OUTSIDE WICK REGULATOR.   PATENT WIND BREAK.

HEIGHT, 16¾ INCHES.

WIDTH, 8¾ INCHES.

DEPTH, 7¼ INCHES.

No. 6.—Square Tubular Lamp with No. 2 Burner and
6-inch Reflector...........................Each, $4 00

One in a box.

NEW IMPROVED SQUARE TUBULAR STREET LAMP.

No. 10.

OUTSIDE WICK REGULATOR.

AUTOMATIC EXTINGUISHER.

PATENT WIND BREAK.   1½ INCH WICK.

No. 10.—Improved Square Tubular Street Lamp......Each, $7 30

One in a box.

Lanterns and Lamps
FOR EVERY PURPOSE

Why bother with an old worn out lantern that is always giving you trouble when for a little money you can buy a Ham Lantern, one that is a pleasure to use and you can always depend on? Ham's Lanterns are strongly made of the very best heavy IX "AA" tin, the burning qualities are excellent, every lamp is thoroughly tested before leaving our factory and all are guaranteed to give perfect satisfaction. Our (Cold Blast) Lanterns are guaranteed not to blow out in the strongest winds. In buying a lantern be sure and ask for Ham's and see that our name is on it. "Take no substitute." If your dealer cannot supply you, write us direct. Address Dept. "T."

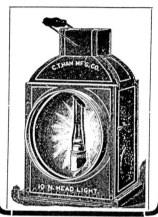

Ham's 10-inch Traction Headlight

Every Thresherman should own a good headlight. It means the saving of a great deal of valuable time and time is money in the threshing season. Very often an hour's work after dark would finish a job, then you could pack up and move your outfit with perfect safety and be all ready for the next job in the morning. This can be accomplished with the aid of a good headlight.

Ham's Headlight is the best on the market. It is built of the very best material, has regular locomotive headlight style of burner and throws an immense volume of bright light, penetrating the darkness much further than ordinary headlights. It will not smoke and is guaranteed not to blow or jar out. You run no risk when you buy a Ham Lamp as they are guaranteed to give perfect satisfaction.

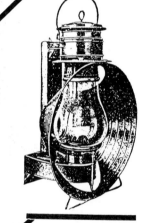

Ham's No. 9 Hanging Lamp "Cold Blast"

Ham's No. 40 Search-Light "Cold Blast."

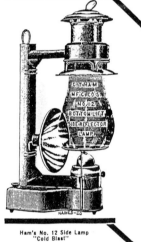

Ham's No. 9 Street Lamp "Cold Blast"

Ham's No. 12 Side Lamp "Cold Blast"

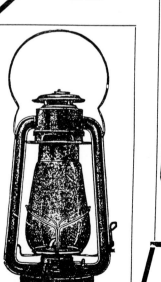

Ham's No. 2 "Cold Blast" Lantern

Ham's No. 0 Clipper Lantern

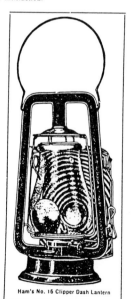

Ham's No. 15 Clipper Dash Lantern

Ham's No. 17 "Cold Blast" Dash Lantern

C. T. Ham Mfg. Co.
ROCHESTER, NEW YORK

TO THE TRADE.

WAIT FOR IT!

Entirely New — "Slickest thing Out."

**PATENT
APPLIED FOR.**

No. 0, Oval Tube **S**ide **S**pring **S**afety
Tubular Lantern.

PERFECT IN ITS OPERATION.

GLASS FLANGE AND BURNER SECURELY
LOCKED. GLOBE REMOVABLE WITH-
OUT TAKING OFF GUARD.

No Springs to Handle.   Automatic when Raised and Lowered.

WE WILL SOON SHOW IT UP.

C. T. HAM MANUFACTURING CO.,

Sole Manufacturers, ROCHESTER, N. Y.

Figure 1927

MILL TUBULAR
LANTERNS

No. 0 – Globe, 1" "B" Wick.
Without Lock. For use of
watchmen in mills. Thor-
oughly guarded, to prevent
breakage of globe. Lantern
cannot be opened while being
used in making rounds.

MOTOR BOAT LIGHTS
SIDE AND BOW LIGHTS—TRIPLEX OR FRESNAL GLASS
Class 3—Boats 40 to 65 Feet in Length

We list herewith a cut of our Special new style set of Fresnal Glass lanterns for this class. The frames are designed in such a way as to make a neat and not clumsy lantern while the Fresnal lenses have more than the correct number of square inches to cover the regulations.

Fig. 716	Fig. 716

No. of square inches required—25.

		Size Glass in Clear	Square Inches	Galvanized Iron Pair	Brass Pair
No. 300	Side Lights	5¾″×5¼″	30″	$6 75	$9 75

BOW LIGHTS
TRIPLEX OR FRESNAL GLASS

Fig. 717

No. of square inches required—31.

		Size Glass in Clear	Number Square Inches	Galvanized Iron Each	Brass Each
No. 301	Bow Lights	4½″×7¾″	35″	$5 25	$9 00

No Rivets used in the construction of the bodies of these lanterns; made same as Class 2.

FRESNAL ANCHOR OR STERN LIGHTS
Same as for Class 2
For Extra Glass Globes see page 248.

MOTOR BOAT LIGHTS

SIDE LIGHTS—TRIPLEX OR FRESNAL GLASS

CLASS 2 BOATS

26 to 39 Ft. in Length

Number of square inches required—16

The illustrations shown are cuts of our Fresnal lenses, lights made in several sizes.

The correct set for class 2 being as follows:

STARBOARD
Fig. 713

PORT
Fig. 713

	Size Glass Clear	Number Square Inch	Galvanized Iron Pair	Brass Pair
No. 200 Side Lights	4″×5″	20	$6 50	$9 50

BOW LIGHTS—TRIPLEX OR FRESNAL GLASS

CLASS 2 BOATS

Number of square inches required—19

	Size Glass	Square Inch	Galvanized Iron Each	Brass Each
No. 201 Bow	4″×7½″	30	$5 00	$6 75

BOW
Fig. 714

ANOTHER NEW FEATURE

There are no rivets used in the construction of the bodies of above lamps, thus making a more solid built lamp than the riveted.

FRESNAL ANCHOR OR STERN LIGHTS

TRIPLEX OR FRESNAL GLASS

Special for Class 2 or 3

Made specially for this class of Boats and match same to a nicety regarding size and diameter of glass.

Fig. 715

	Diameter of Glass	Height of Glass	Height Frame	Extreme Height	Galvanized Each	Polished Brass Each
No. 202	4¾″	4¼″	10	14	$3 00	$5 00

For Extra Glass Globes see page 248.

Dark Lanterns.

No. **10**.—Japanned, 2½ inch Lens, 7 inches high.... Per dozen, $5 50

No. **20**.— "   3 "   " 8 "   "   "   ..... "   6 75

Tin Tubular Lanterns.

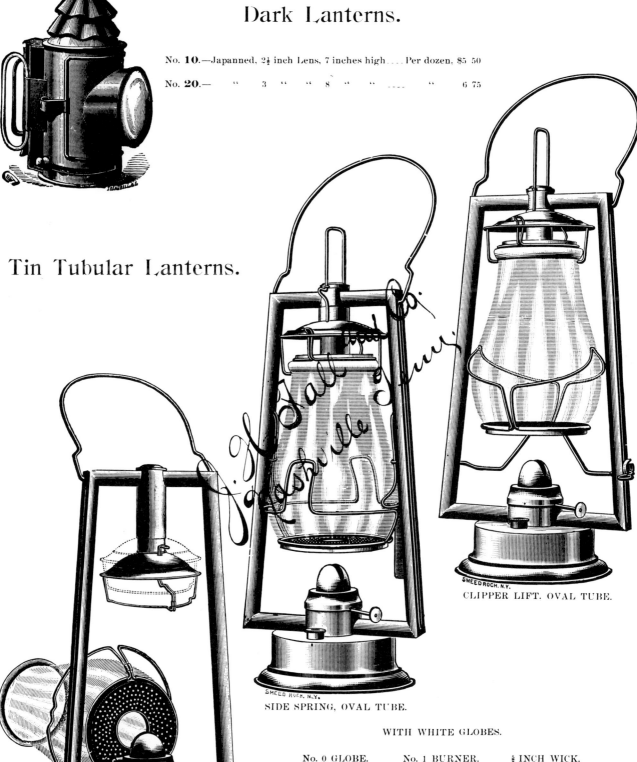

CLIPPER LIFT. OVAL TUBE.

SIDE SPRING, OVAL TUBE.

LEADER TUBULAR.

WITH WHITE GLOBES.

No. 0 GLOBE.   No. 1 BURNER.   ⅝ INCH WICK.

No. **0**.—Clipper Lift, Oval Tube Lanterns ....Per dozen, $6 50

No. **0**.—Improved Side Spring, Oval Tube Lanterns ..... "   6 50

No. **0**.—Leader Tubular Lanterns.................... "   6 30

One dozen in a box.

The Gem Driving Lamp.
IMPROVED.

This is absolutely the best and most scientifically constructed driving lamp on the market, or that was ever made. So many driving lamps have been presented to the public as "first class" in their burning qualities and have turned out to be worthless things, that we take a justifiable pride in claiming for the Gem the following points: That it is superior in construction and finish, that it is a perfect lantern in its burning qualities, the light produced is stronger and brighter than the light produced by any lamp using a ½ inch burner, it will not smoke or blow out, nor is it possible to jar it out over rough roads; the reflector is conical, like those used on locomotive headlights, and is of solid copper, heavily silver plated, the lens is extra thick and of the best quality plate glass, with beveled edge. So confident are we of the merits of the Gem that should any purchaser find or prove after using that they are not exactly as represented by us, they may be returned and money will be cheerfully refunded. 55750. Brass.........$2.50

55752 Nickel plated....................... 3.00
55753 Japan finish to match dash and finish of buggy or coach. Each....................... 2.45
55754 Clamps for fastening Gem Lamp to dash. Each $0.25

55756 Seat Rod Bracket for fitting Gem Lamp to upright rod at end of seat. Each.$0.25

IT'S ALL IN THE TURN

THE CASEY LANTERNS

Indispensable to Trainmen and Boatmen

Because the light is under control from outside the globe without necessity for removing oil cup, and by action of the whole hand. The manipulation of the light is not dependent upon the use of a small finger-and-thumb disc. When gloved or when numbed by cold, the complete hand can do easily with the "Casey" device, what the finger-and-thumb find difficult, in regulating the light in the old-fashioned lantern.

Price per dozen........................$12.00

Figure 1923

COLD BLAST TIN DASH LAMP

Round Tube, Clipper Lift, With Bull's Eye

No. 2 Cold Blast Burner. 1" "B" Wick. No. 0 Cold Blast Globe.
Finished in Blue Japanned.

No. 320.—Japanned and B. E. Globe Price per dozen, $20.50

CLIPPER TUBULAR LANTERNS

Clipper Lift No. 0

No. 0 Globe. ⅝" "A" Wick. Locked Burner. Inside Guard. Quickly raised and lowered. Oil Fount retinned. Furnished in the following styles:

No. 0 Tin White Globe..........	Price per dozen,		$ 9.50
" Red "	"	" "	11.00
Brass White, "	"	" "	30.00
Brass Red "	"	" "	31.50

Figure 1924

BICYCLE LAMPS.

LIGHTWEIGHT.

Light Weight, · · · · each $1 00

Height 5½ in., 2½ in. lens, brass and steel, heavily coated with copper and nickel plated, no solder, burns kerosene.
ONE IN A BOX.

JIM DANDY.

Jim Dandy, · · · · each $1.25

Nickel plated, removable top, hinged bottom, 2¼ in. ground lens, hinged front, ruby and green side lights, packed reservoir, removable reflector, rigid bracket, height 5½ in., burns kerosene.
ONE IN A BOX

BANNER.

Banner, · · · · each $2.50

Brass, riveted and nickel plated, removable top, reflector and burner, removable and reversible oil pot, locking device holds wick firmly in position, 3 in. double convex ground lens, ball and socket joint, permitting adjustment to any angle, only bracket of the kind, height 6 in.
ONE IN A BOX.

I. C.

I. C., · · · · each $1.00

Weight 11 oz., all parts brass, riveted and heavily nickel plated, can be cleaned and reassembled in one minute, burns kerosene.
ONE IN A BOX.

EVERLIT.

Everlit, · · · · each $1.50

Nickel plated, hinged front door, 2½ in convex lens, height 5¾ in., weight 13 oz., burns kerosene
ONE IN A BOX

DIETZ.

Dietz, · · · · each $2.50

Brass, polished and nickel plated, weight 12 oz., no solder, except on bottom of oil fount, parabolic reflector, throwing rays of light straight ahead, packed oil fount, wick will not jar down, hinged front door.
ONE IN A BOX.

BICYCLE LAMPS.

SOLAR ACETYLENE GAS.

Solar Acetylene Gas, - - - each $3.50

The manufacturers of this lamp were the first on the field. They control many special features to be found in no other lamp. They offer several improvements over last year's model. It is lighter, and is more symmetrical in appearance, has removable tip holder, water feed greatly improved.

M. & W. LANCASTER ACETYLENE GAS.

M. & W. Lancaster Acetylene Gas, each $3.00

All parts brass, nickel plated, combination bracket for head or fork, burns carbide in any form, exposed parts always cold. Combination water and gas cock, by the same turn of the cock the water and gas are both turned off preserving the gas for future use. Therefore it is not necessary to turn off the water before wishing to dispense with the light. ¼ ft. fishtail burner, throws light 100 ft. ahead and 50 ft. wide. With a full charge the lamp will burn over five hours.

BRECKENRIDGE ACETYLENE GAS.

Breckenridge Acetylene Gas, - each $3.50

Made entirely of heavy gauge brass, handsomely nickel plated, weighs 2 lbs. when filled, ready to light. Removable aluminum reflector and top. 2½ inch double convex French lens, hinged lens holder, large colored prism side lights. Removable aluminum carbide chamber. ¼ ft. fish tail burner, lava tip, 125 candle power, which throws a very brilliant light 75 to 100 ft. ahead of the wheel angle of radiation 60 degrees, will burn about 4 hours with 3 or 3½ oz. of calcium carbide and 4 oz. of water. Adjustable rigid bracket.

20TH CENTURY ACETYLENE GAS.

20th Century Acetylene Gas, - each $3.50

Made of brass and steel, nickel plated, aluminum parabolic reflector, hinged front door and red and green side lights, uses any granulated carbide, burns full flame from six to eight hours.

BICYCLE LAMPS.

THE M. & W.

M. & W., · · · · each $3.00

Brass, nickel plated, burns kerosene, reversible oil pot with improved lock, fine ground 2½ in. lens, improved wick lock, released by pressing on end of button, height 5½ in.

20TH CENTURY.

20th Century, · · · each $2.50

Brass, nickel plated, burns kerosene; self-locking wick, improved locking device for oil fount, aluminum parabolic reflector, hinged front and side doors, rigid bracket.

SEARCHLIGHT.

Searchlight, · · · · each $4.00

Extra heavy and strong, richly embossed, burns kerosene.

HAM'S DIAMOND.

Diamond, · · · · each $3.00

Steel, heavily nickel plated, constructed on the tubular principle, burns kerosene, 2½ in. double convex lens, double ratchet burner, rigid bracket, height 6 in.

X RAYS.

X Rays, · · · · each $3.00

Aluminum, colored side lights, each lamp is provided with high and low cap, positive wick locking device attached to each ratchet button to lock wick from either side, sheet steel bracket, heavily nickel plated, weight, including bracket, 16 oz., height 7½ in.

Early Tole Wristlet
Candle Lantern.

Six Sided Presentation
Lantern, made by
Gleason & Bailey.

Dietz Fire King Lantern,
nickel plated, clear globe.

Dietz Fire King Lantern,
polished brass, with ruby globe.

Chief's Lantern, polished
brass, clear globe, by Peter
Gray of Boston.

Wrist Lantern,
nickel plated, used
on a steam fire
engine, made by
W. Porter & Sons,
1880's.

Brass Chief's Lantern, note
the large bail handle.

Left - Ham Lantern, nickel plated, ruby
globe, 1905.
Right - Dietz Fire Queen Lantern, nickel
plated, clear globe, 1905.

Pair of Dietz Coldblast Lanterns, polished
brass, 1920.

Brass Wrist Lantern
with ruby globe.

Eclipse Presentation Lantern, nickel plated.

Eclipse Lantern, nickel
plated with replacement
globe.

Brass Wrist Lantern, red &
clear glass with "Chief
Engineer" etched in globe,
made by William Porter &
Sons, New York, 1880's.

123,982

UNITED STATES PATENT OFFICE.

JOSEPH S. DENNIS, OF CHICAGO, ILLINOIS.

IMPROVEMENT IN TUBULAR LANTERNS.

Specification forming part of Letters Patent No. 123,982, dated February 27, 1872.

Specification describing certain Improvements in Tubular Lanterns, invented by JOSEPH S. DENNIS, of Chicago, in the county of Cook and State of Illinois.

This invention relates to an improvement in the construction of that class of lanterns well known to the art as "tubular lanterns;" and the invention consists especially in the construction and arrangement of the bell or receiver placed above the flame in connection with the side tubes; the said receiver or bell being extended laterally in the present invention, and attached by proper means to the said side tubes, thus adding greatly to the strength and durability of the lantern.

In the accompanying drawing, Figure 1 represents a front elevation of a tubular lantern embodying my improvement; and Fig. 2, a horizontal section of Fig. 1 on the line x x, looking downward.

Like letters of reference made use of in the several figures indicate like parts.

General Description.

A is the base of the lantern; B, the globe or protector; and C, the receiver or bell, placed above the globe, and communicating with the short central vertical tube D, to the upper extremity of which are attached the pair of descending tubes E E, re-entering at the base of the lantern. The bell C is attached to the bottom of the tube D, being commonly soldered thereto. To this bell, or, as is sometimes the case, to the tube D, is attached the spring device for retaining the globe in position by means of a downward pressure exerted from the tube or bell through the spring and upon the globe at its upper rim, and necessarily with some force.

When the globe-holding spring is to be released, more or less lateral pressure occurs, especially when the style shown in the drawing is used, tending to push the bell out from between the tubes E, straining and loosening the joints, and tending ultimately, by the torsion thus produced, to destroy the integrity of the joints at the juncture of the tube D with the tubes E, and tending to crimp and loosen the bell C from the tube D. To obviate this tendency, the metal straps a a are soldered or otherwise attached to the sides of the bell C, and extended out and connected to the tubes E E upon each side. By this simple device a perfect bracing of the entire upper portion of the lantern is effected, and the difficulty hitherto existing entirely done away with.

An equivalent to the employment of the separate straps or pieces a a would be the extension of the bell itself so as to reach the tubes and be joined thereto, and I contemplate so attaching the bell, either by enlarging the entire diameter thereof, or by making it of a greater diameter in one direction than another.

Claim.

Having thus fully described my invention, what I claim, and desire to secure by Letters Patent, is—

The combination of the bell C and tubes E E of a tubular lantern, when the bell is attached laterally to the tubes, in the manner substantially as specified and shown.

J. S. DENNIS.

Witnesses:
  JOHN W. MUNDAY,
  HEINR. F. BRUNS.

JOSEPH S. DENNIS.

Tubular Lantern.

No. 123,982.

Patented Feb. 27, 1872.

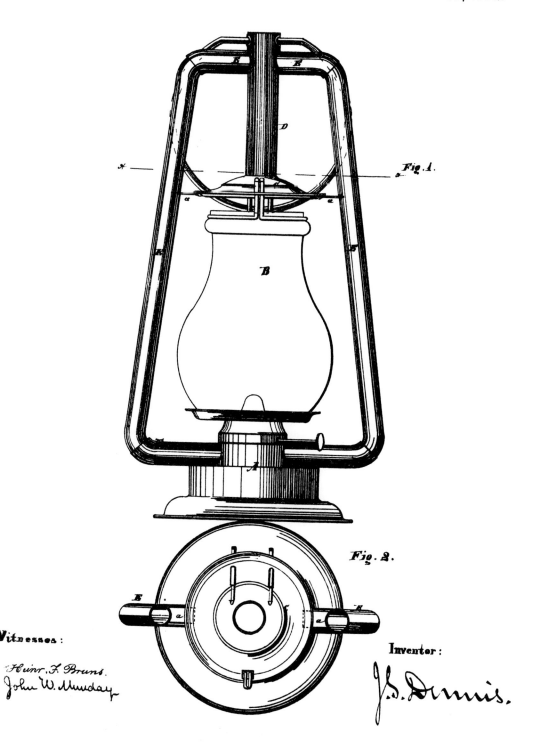

Fig.1.

Fig.2.

Witnesses:

Heinr. F. Bruns.
John W. Munday

Inventer:

J. S. Dennis.

124,181

UNITED STATES PATENT OFFICE.

HARTSHORN WHITE, OF PHILLIPSBURG, NEW JERSEY.

IMPROVEMENT IN SIGNAL-LIGHTS.

Specification forming part of Letters Patent No. 124,181, dated February 27, 1872.

SPECIFICATION.

To all whom it may concern:

Be it known that I, H. WHITE, of Phillipsburg, in the county of Warren and State of New Jersey, have invented certain new and useful Improvements in Head-Lights for Locomotives; and I do hereby declare that the following is a full, clear, and exact description thereof, reference being had to the accompanying drawing and to the letters of reference marked thereon which form a part of this specification.

The nature of my invention consists in combining with a no-colored chimney of a head-signal or calcium light, a movable exterior colored chimney; and also in combining with said no-colored and colored chimneys a movable exterior metallic or opaque chimney, as will be hereinafter more fully set forth.

In order to enable others skilled in the art to which my invention appertains to make and use the same, I will now proceed to describe its construction and operation referring to the annexed drawing, in which—

Figure 1 is a front view of a locomotive head-light or reflector and lamp, and Fig. 2 is a vertical section of Fig. 1 taken on the line *x x*.

A represents the reflector of a locomotive head-light, and B represents the base or support of the usual no-colored chimney C. In all head-lights the lamp is placed in the back part of the reflector, so that the rays of light from the flame will strike on nearly every part of its polished surface. The focus is such that a flood of light is thus thrown upon the railroad object. E represents a colored chimney or tube, so arranged upon the outside of the no-colored chimney that it can be lowered below the flame or raised to surround the same, the object being in the latter case to color the rays of the head-lamp before they come in contact with the reflector, and thus display a bright but colored light when danger is to be signaled.

On some railroads red lights are used to indicate danger; others use green; and still others use blue; hence the color is not material, as any desired color may be used; and I may use more than one of said colored tubes or chimneys of different colors, as sometimes one color is used to denote danger while another denotes caution. I also use an independent movable metallic or opaque chimney or ring, D, whereby the reflector may be entirely eclipsed by simply raising the same so as to surround the flame, it having the same motion as the colored chimney. This metallic chimney or ring is to be used at night when two or more trains are moving south or east and should meet with a train moving north or west, (as the course of the road may be,) the head-light rays on the locomotive moving north or west will cover and destroy all signal-lights on rear of train No. 1 moving south or east, from view of the engineer of train No. 2 moving in the same direction, and renders the head-light of engine (train moving north or west) a positive nuisance; but by moving the independent movable metallic chimney the engineer can partially or totally eclipse his head-lamp so that the opposing engineer can have full view.

It is also, when not in use, of great advantage and benefit, in that it stands immediately around the colored chimney to shield the same from the rays of light being reflected upon it, which would partially destroy the strength or power of the rays of the head-light. The metallic or opaque chimney may also be used as a signal, and should in all cases be silver-plated or burnished. The arrangement of the colored and metallic chimneys may be used in the same manner on stationary signal-lights and on calcium-lights for artificial purposes. The movable chimneys may be operated in various ways. In the present case a rack, *a*, and pinion *b* is actuated by means of gearing F and crank G. A connecting-rod should extend back to the "cab," so as to be always within reach of the engineer, who will operate the chimneys when necessary. The metallic or opaque chimney D may be operated by a similar device, or by a lever, H, as shown in the drawing. The means for operating the movable chimneys are, however, immaterial, only so that they can be raised and lowered at the will of the engineer.

H. WHITE.

Improvement in Signal Lights.

No. 124,181.   Patented Feb. 27, 1872.

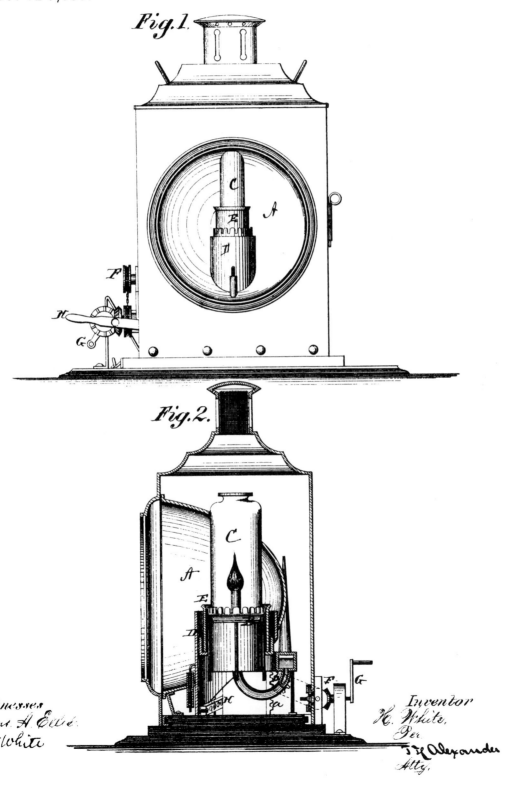

Fig.1.

Fig.2.

Witnesses   Inventor
Jns. H. Ebbs.   H. White.
F. White   Per
                                            T. H. Alexander
                                            Atty.

124,372

UNITED STATES PATENT OFFICE.

GEORGE MORTIMER, OF JERSEY CITY HEIGHTS, NEW JERSEY.

IMPROVEMENT IN LANTERNS.

Specification forming part of Letters Patent No. 124,372, dated March 5, 1872.

To all whom it may concern:

Be it known that I, GEORGE MORTIMER, of Jersey City Heights, in the county of Hudson and State of New Jersey, have invented a new and useful Improvement in Lanterns; and I do hereby declare the following to be a full, clear, and exact description thereof, which will enable those skilled in the art to make and use the same, reference being had to the accompanying drawing forming part of this specification, in which drawing—

Figure 1 is a vertical central section of my improvement. Fig. 2 is a horizontal section taken in the plane of the line *x x* of Fig. 1.

Similar letters indicate corresponding parts.

This invention relates to lanterns, and is designed for such as are portable, though it can be used with others; and it consists in forming or providing the globe where it comes in contact with the metal frame that incloses and holds it with projecting zones of suitable width to enable the globe to be held steadily by the rings of the frame.

The letter A designates a glass globe of a hand-lantern, and B the pedestal of the metallic frame by which it is inclosed. The vessel C or "lamp" proper, which contains the oil and wick, is inserted from below, and is secured in place by means of spring catches D D, fastened on opposite sides of the vessel, and which work in slots made in its lower rim, E, and are made with square shoulders that catch over the inside flange F of the pedestal when the vessel reaches its proper position in the interior of the pedestal. The bottom edge of the glass globe enters the vertical part of the pedestal and rests on the stops G, formed on its inner surface, as is illustrated in Fig. 1, which stops are above the line of the air openings H made through the sides of the pedestal, so that the sides of the globe will not interrupt the entrance of air to support combustion. In order to prevent the flame of the lamp from being put out by the sudden rush of air when the lantern is lowered, or by any other violent current of inrushing air, I form a curtain, I, above the line of air-openings H, consisting of an annular rim that projects from the upper part of the "lamp" C, toward the sides of the globe, so as to leave a narrow open space between the edge of the curtain and the sides of the globe, through which a thin uninterrupted stream of air can pass upward to the flame. The curtain I arrests air which rushes in with too great violence, and forms the upper wall of an annular air-space of which the lower rim E forms the lower wall, in which space the inrushing air has room for circulation. The letter J designates the metal cap of the lantern perforated to allow the products of combustion to escape, and the interior is provided with projections, K K, which serve to fasten the cap to the globe by passing down through vertical grooves L L, which extend downward from the upper edge of the globe until they intersect a horizontal groove, M, into which the projections are passed by rotating the cap.

The frame of the lantern above the pedestal consists of a flat ring or band, N, in whose inner side half-round recesses O are made to receive the upper ends of the vertical bars P of the frame, which are soldered, or otherwise suitably fastened, in the recesses. Like recesses are made for the lower ends of said bars in the inner side of the ring Q, which forms the upper part of the pedestal, where said lower ends are also fastened by soldering. The vertical bars are crimped inwardly, as seen at R, in the same horizontal line to receive a guard-wire or ring, S, which goes around outside all the vertical bars, and, its ends being fastened together, it is retained in place by the crimp without other fastening. The globe is held in the frame of the lantern by the top and bottom rings N Q; and in order to present to them a suitable holding-surface, I form projecting zones, T T, at those parts of the globe which come opposite to the rings, the bottom zone forming the lower edge of the globe. These zones have vertical sides to conform to the inner sides of the rings, and thereby present good bearing surfaces where the globe and rings come in contact. Another advantage of the upper zone T is that it enables me to make the ring N of a sufficient diameter to allow the globe to be inserted into the frame from above.

What I claim as new, and desire to secure by Letters Patent, is—

The vertical projecting zones T of the globe, in combination with the rings N Q of the frame, substantially as described.

Witnesses: GEORGE MORTIMER.

W. HAUFF,

E. F. KASTENHUBER.

GEORGE MORTIMER.
Lantern.

No. 124,372.   Patented March 5, 1872.

Fig. 1.

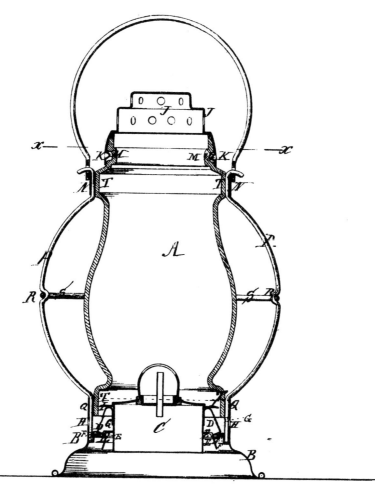

Fig. 2.

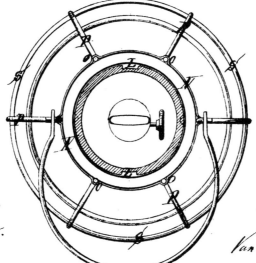

Witnesses
E. F. Kastenhuber.
Ernst Bilhuber.

Inventor.
George Mortimer
pr
Van Santvoord & Hauff
attys

123,208

UNITED STATES PATENT OFFICE.

CHARLES J. SYKES, OF CHICAGO, ILLINOIS.

IMPROVEMENT IN LANTERNS.

Specification forming part of Letters Patent No. 122,208, dated January 30, 1872.

SPECIFICATION.

I, CHARLES J. SYKES, of Chicago, in the county of Cook and State of Illinois, have invented a new and useful Improvement in Lanterns, of which the following is a specification, reference being had to the accompanying drawing.

Nature and Object of my Invention.

My invention relates to that class of hand-lanterns known as removable-globe lanterns; and it consists in a novel construction of the band C C and a novel mode of attaching the vertical wires B B, which are a portion of the guard-wires, to the band C C, through which the globe passes in the operation of its removal from the lantern.

Description of the Drawing.

Figure 1 represents a vertical sectional view of what is known as an open-top lantern, showing my band C C and tip E; and Fig. 2 represents a side elevation of an open-bottom lantern, showing my band C C and tip E, as there applied; and Fig. 3 represents a detached view of my tip E for fastening the guard-wires B B to the band C C in the form in which it is cut from the metal; and Fig. 4 represents a transverse sectional view of my band C C, with a modified form of my tip E attached thereto when the band is bent in a circular form, and showing the guard-wires B B when fastened in their places by the tip; and Fig. 5 represents a side elevation of the same parts when attached, before they are bent in a circular form, the guard-wires B B excepted; and Fig. 6 represents a side elevation of another modification of my tip E.

General Description.

A represents any ordinary base of a hand-lantern, made in any of the known forms, with the oil-fountain secured therein in any desirable manner. B B are the upright guard-wires in Fig. 1, in the usual form for an open-top lantern; and in Fig. 2 in the usual form for an open-bottom lantern. C is my new band, made of metal, and it is sufficiently large in diameter for the globe to pass through it. When the band C is made of sheet metal it is turned upon one edge so that a flange is formed, upon which the ends of the guard-wires B B may rest in an open-bottom lantern, and which rests upon the ends of said guard-wires in open-top lanterns, by means of which flange I am also enabled to securely and easily fasten said band to the top or base, respectively, of each kind of lanterns. E E represent what I term my T-shaped tip to distinguish it from the modification of the tip hereafter described. In Fig. 3 the dotted lines represent cuts through the metal of my tip, forming what may be termed the leaves of my tip, where made in this form. In order to fasten the upright guard-wires B B to the band c, the tip is placed in its proper place upon the band, so that its leaves may be turned around the ends of the upright guard-wires, and so that it will rest against the flange of the band c as well as the side of said band. The leaves of the tips being turned around the ends of the upright guard-wires, the tip is then soldered to the band, and the guard-wires mentioned are soldered to the tip and to the band. It will be observed that I am able, by this means, to fasten the upright guard-wires very firmly to the band. The modification of my tip may be described as follows: It is evident that the use of the tip already described would require as many separate tips for the purpose intended as there are upright guard-wires, while Fig. 6 represents my continuous tip, with the leaves of the tip cut through projections left at proper intervals upon the edge thereof, as shown, and this constitutes one of the modified forms of my tip. Another modification of my tip is represented in Fig. 5. The tip there shown having neither projections nor leaves it may be termed a straight and continuous tip. This tip is represented in Fig. 6 as being in its place upon the band c in open-top lanterns, and it is made to conform as nearly as may be to the ends of the upright guard-wires B B, as shown at F F in Figs. 4 and 5. The band c is also shown at D D, in Fig. 4, as half-encircling the ends of the guards B B.

Having described the nature and construction of my invention, what I claim, and desire to secure by Letters Patent, is—

The combination of the band C and tip E, when constructed as and for the purposes specified and shown.

C. J. SYKES.

Witnesses:
FRANCIS F. WARNER,
HEINR. T. BRUNS.

C. J. SYKES.

Lantern.

No. 123,208.

Patented Jan. 30, 1872.

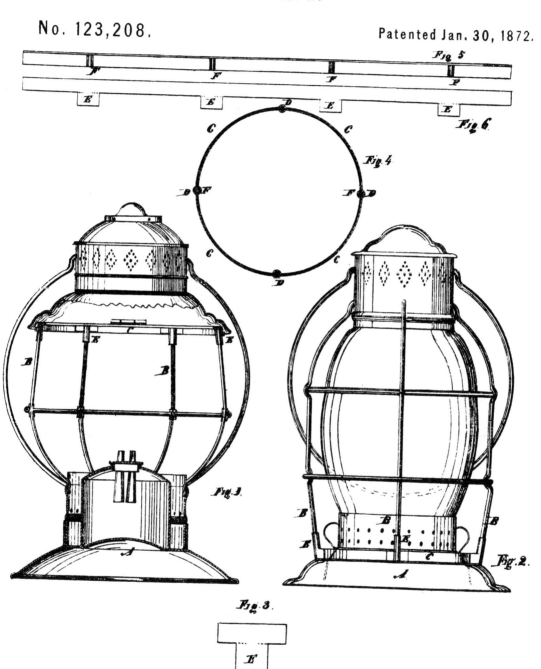

Witnesses:
Heinrich F. Bruns.
Francis F. Warner.

Inventor:
Charles J. Sykes
by Lewis L. Coburn
atty.

122,931

UNITED STATES PATENT OFFICE.

CHARLES S. S. BARON, OF BELLAIRE, OHIO.

IMPROVEMENT IN LANTERNS.

Specification forming part of Letters Patent No. 122,931, dated January 23, 1872.

To all whom it may concern:

Be it known that I, CHARLES S. S. BARON, of Bellaire, in the county of Belmont and State of Ohio, have invented a new and useful Improvement in Lanterns, of which the following is a specification:

My invention relates more especially to that class of lanterns known as railroad lanterns; and my said invention consists in constructing the guard-tubes connecting the cap with the base of a lantern of distinct, separable sections, the upper sections fitting within and sliding into the lower sections, the two thus interlocking being held to each other so as to firmly hold the globe between the cap and base, and admit of its instant removal for cleansing and lighting the lamp; and further, in the arrangement of a bow-spring, secured to the band of the base centrally between its bent and beveled ends, which are free to enter or be withdrawn from slots or mortises formed in both sections of tubes, in such manner that when the ends of the upper sections of tubes enter the lower sections they will automatically compress the spring through its beveled bent ends until the slots in both sections of tubes match each other, when the ends of the spring, being released from contact with the ends of the upper sections of tubes, enter both slots, and thus firmly hold the interlocking sections; the spring being so arranged as to be readily operated by two fingers of one hand to release the ends from the slots, and thus allow the sections to be separated, while their interlocking is accomplished automatically.

In the accompanying drawing, Figure 1 represents a side elevation of a lantern embracing my invention. Fig. 2 represents a similar view, the globe being removed and the connecting guard-tubes separated from each other. Fig. 3 represents a vertical central section of Fig. 1; and Fig. 4 represents a horizontal section in line x x of Fig. 1.

The ordinary cup a, foot b, and perforated band c are formed in the usual manner of sheet metal, and at opposite sides of the band short tubes d are soldered to the foot a, in vertical positions, and braced to the band c by braces d'. To the reflector f of the dome g are soldered, at corresponding points, tubes e, extending downwardly, and of a little less diameter than the tubes d, so as to enable them to be slid into the tubes d when the parts are put together. The tubes d and e are slotted or mortised, as shown at h, the slots or mortises of both sets of tubes matching with each other when the parts are put together to allow the bent ends i of a flat spring, j, to enter said slots or mortises h, whereby the tubes e are prevented from slipping out of the tubes d unless the spring be so compressed toward the periphery of the band c, as to withdraw the bent ends i from the slots or mortises h, which is easily accomplished by reason of the central connection of said spring. The globe k rests on the band c, its lower end m extending into the same, and its upper narrow straight end l extends into the dome g in such a manner that, when the parts are put together as shown in Figs. 1 and 3, the globe is held firmly between the dome g and band c, and can be removed only by compressing spring j to remove its ends i from the slots or mortises h, and elevating the dome g with its reflector f and tubes e from the tubes d of the foot. The ends of springs j, which are, as above described, bent at i, pass through slots j' in braces d', so as to prevent any downward movement of the ends of the spring under the pressure of the tubes e upon them while interlocking the parts. Thus the slots j' act as braces to the spring, insuring the entrance of its ends i into the slots or mortises h of tubes e without fail every time the tubes e are depressed into the tubes d. The usual bail or handle n is suitably pivoted to the dome g. The tubes d e, when the parts are put together, not only unite the several parts in connection with spring j, which holds them together firmly, but also serve as guards for the protection of the globe. The beveled upper edges of the ends i of spring j allow of the automatic interlocking of tubes e and d by merely depressing the former into the latter until the ends i can pass through the slots h in both, while the straight lower edge of the ends i prevents any accidental removal of the ends from the slots unless the spring j is compressed from outside.

To enable manufacturers to make a low-priced lantern with a removable globe guarded with wire in the usual manner, they must construct the parts of flimsy material, thereby considerably weakening them; but by my improved

(90.)

C. S. S. BARON.
Lantern.

No. 122,931.

Patented Jan. 23, 1872.

Fig. 1.

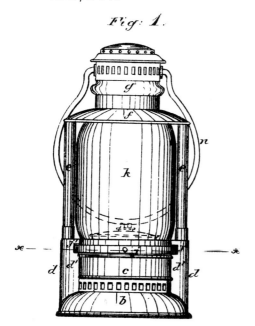

Fig. 2.

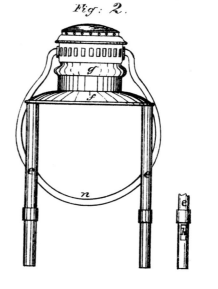

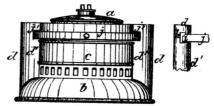

Fig. 3.

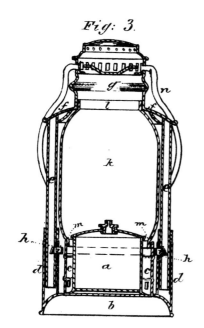

Fig. 4.

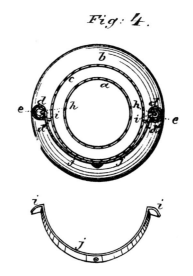

Witnesses:

J. West Magnus.

Parker W. Sweet Jr.

Inventor:

Charles S. S. Baron

by

Johnson Maucke & Co.

his Attorneys

107

121,241

UNITED STATES PATENT OFFICE.

ALONZO FRENCH, OF PHILADELPHIA, PENNSYLVANIA.

IMPROVEMENT IN LANTERNS.

Specification forming part of Letters Patent No. 121,241, dated November 28, 1871.

To all whom it may concern:

Be it known that I, ALONZO FRENCH, of the city and county of Philadelphia, in the State of Pennsylvania, have invented a new and useful Improvement in Lamps and Lanterns; and I do hereby declare the following to be a full, clear, and exact description thereof, which will enable others skilled in the art to which it appertains to make and use my invention, reference being had to the accompanying drawing which forms a part of this specification, and in which—

Figure 1, Sheet 1, represents a lantern containing my improvement; Fig. 2, Sheet 2, a similar lantern, arranged for burning coal-oil; and Fig. 3, Sheet 3, a side light.

The said invention consists in the arrangement of the screw-thread by which the lamp or lantern is attached to its supporting-collar. It also consists in the construction of the skeleton stand.

The same parts are denoted by the same letters in all the figures.

A in the drawing represents the stand or base, which is of open or skeleton form; and consists, usually, of an upper and a lower ring, united by arms *a a*. To the upper ring *b* is secured, in any convenient manner, the oil-fountain B. Between the stand and fountain is the perforated ventilator C, which also forms a rest for the globe D. The globe has a screw-thread, *d d*, formed on its outer surface, by means of which it is securely fastened to the screw-collar E of the guards. This thread may be on any intermediate part of the globe, but must not be at the top or bottom edge thereof. The stand A is constructed with one or more lugs or claws, F, and

with a spring-catch, G, to receive the bottom ring of the guard; and by means of these devices or their equivalents the guard is fastened to the stand. In Fig. 2, which represents a coal-oil lamp, the perforated rest C is arranged above the oil-fountain. Fig. 3 represents a side-light, in which the screw-collar E is attached to a bracket or other stationary support.

I am aware that a screw-thread has been heretofore applied to the top or bottom of a glass-lamp or globe, and to both the top and bottom thereof, for the purpose of supporting the same, by means of a screw-collar. By my improvement, however, the thread being arranged on an intermediate part of the surface, not only is the danger of breaking the glass diminished, but the globe is more steadily supported. The skeleton stand may also be applied to a lamp, in which case it not only prevents the tilting of the lamp, but permits the light to shine without obstruction in a downward direction.

What I claim as my invention, and desire to secure by Letters Patent, is—

1. A screw-thread, arranged on and between the ends of the globe of a lamp or lantern.

2. A detachable skeleton stand for lanterns, constructed with catches or equivalent devices, operating as and for the purpose described.

3. A skeleton stand for lamps or lanterns, constructed so as to be detachable, substantially as above described.

ALONZO FRENCH.

Witnesses:
  M. F. WALTON,
  WM. R. WRIGHT.

(90)

3 Sheets--Sheet 1.

ALONZO FRENCH.

Improvement in Lanterns.

No. 121,241.   Patented Nov. 28, 1871.

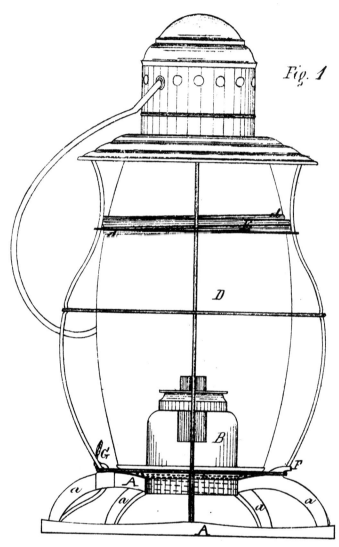

Fig. 1

Witnesses: Inventor.
Wm. R. Wright.   Alonzo French,
Thos. A. Kurtt.   by his Atty,
                                Horace Binney, 3rd.

118,278

UNITED STATES PATENT OFFICE.

WILLIAM S. ROBERTS AND EGBERT H. FISKE, OF EAST GREENWICH, R. I.

IMPROVEMENT IN SIGNAL-LANTERNS.

Specification forming part of Letters Patent No. 118,278, dated August 22, 1871.

To all whom it may concern:

Be it known that we, WILLIAM S. ROBERTS and EGBERT H. FISKE, of East Greenwich, in the county of Kent and State of Rhode Island, have invented certain Improvements in Signal-Lanterns, of which the following is a specification:

Our invention relates more especially to lanterns used on railway trains and for other signal purposes; and its nature consists in making the lantern with two globes, one above the other, the lower one being a duplicate, except in color, of the upper one, but in a reversed position, the whole being hung on sliding pivots formed on the ends of the bail, the lamp inside being hung on pivots so as to retain its proper position when the globes are reversed; the object being to provide a lantern that can be changed instantly from a white light to a colored one or from one color to another.

Figure 1 is a front elevation of the lantern. Fig. 2 is the same with one of the globes removed. Fig. 3 is one of the glass globes. Fig. 4 shows the wire guard-cage that covers the globe.

The center frame A is a ring, made with an upper and lower flange, the outer edges of which are turned over to hold the lower ring of the guard-cage S, and an edge is also made on the inner side of the flange above and below to keep the glass globes *a* in place. S is a guard to protect the globes, and is made of a double plate of metal at one end, to which the wires are fastened, the other ends of the wires being fastened to a wire ring that fits inside the edges of the flanges, and is held securely by a catch on the spring *o*, the catch projecting up through a hole in the flange, so as to come inside of the ring and project out over it. A bracket, *d*, is attached to each side of the lantern, the ends being curved in and fastened to the flanges of the middle frame A. These brackets have slots cut in them nearly the whole length to receive the ends of the bail C, which are turned square in through the brackets and headed on the inside to hold them in, the object of the slots in the brackets being to allow the lantern to slide down on the bail when reversed, so that the center of gravity will be below the points of suspension, in order to keep the lantern upright. B is the lamp, which is held by the pivots *x x* placed above the center of gravity, that the lamp may keep its proper vertical position when the outside case of the lantern is turned over. The glass globes *a*, Fig. 3, are alike in shape, but it is intended to have one of clear glass and the other of colored glass, or both of colored glass, but of different colors, so that by holding the lantern by the bail C and turning the lantern over on the pivots in the brackets a different-colored light will be produced, avoiding the necessity of having another lantern and enabling a person to make the change instantly when a danger or other signal is wanted, without loss of time that may be dangerous.

What we claim as our invention is—

1. The combination of the two globes *a* and guards S with the swinging lamp B, substantially as and for the purpose specified.

2. The combination of the bail C and slotted brackets *d d* with the reversible lantern, substantially as herein set forth, and for the purpose stated.

WILLIAM S. ROBERTS.
EGBERT H. FISKE.

Witnesses:
THOMAS J. TILLEY,
A. V. DAWLY.

WILLIAM S. ROBERTS & EGBERT H. FISKE.

Improvement in Signal-Lanterns.

No. 118,278. Patented Aug. 22, 1871.

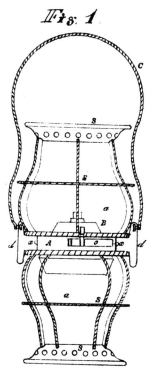

Fig. 1. Fig. 2. Fig. 3. Fig. 4.

Witnesses

Thomas Tilley
A. V. Dandy

Inventors

William S Roberts
Egbert H. Fiske

AM. PHOTO-LITHOGRAPHIC CO. N.Y. (OSBORNE'S PROCESS.)

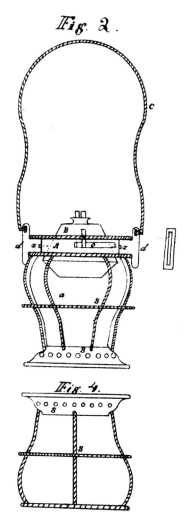

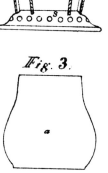

123,981

UNITED STATES PATENT OFFICE.

JOSEPH S. DENNIS, OF CHICAGO, ILLINOIS.

IMPROVEMENT IN TUBULAR LANTERNS.

Specification forming part of Letters Patent No. 123,981, dated February 27, 1872.

Specification describing certain Improvements in the Construction of Tubular Lanterns, invented by JOSEPH S. DENNIS, of Chicago, in the county of Cook and State of Illinois.

This invention relates to an improvement in the construction of that style of lantern well known to the art as the tubular lantern; and it especially appertains to the construction of the air-chamber below the cone of the burner of such lanterns. This chamber surrounds the neck of the oil-pot and lower portion of the burner and wick-tube, being of cylindrical shape, and consisting of a vertical annular band or wall, at the sides of which enter the air-tubes for conveying air for combustion to the burner, and fitted at top to receive the overlapping lower edge of the cone of the burner. Hitherto this chamber has been made of a band or strip of tin bent or rolled into shape and having the ends soldered together, making a vertical seam at one side where joined. It has been impossible on account of this seam, which produces a ridge, to make the cone fit down over the edge of the chamber so closely as to exclude the air; and it has also been found that, where the chamber is made of such a strip so soldered, it is practically impossible to make the chambers all of a given diameter, the variation being likely to occur in the holding, soldering, or bending in the process of manufacture. And the present invention consists in making this air-chamber, or rather the vertical wall thereof, of a continuous sheet of tin, stamped out of the metal into the desired form, whereby a regular form is produced, never varying in size, and entirely without the objectionable side seam, and whereby a regular and even taper may be given to the upper end of said chamber, and a perfect fit insured for the overlapping edge of the cone.

In the accompanying drawing, Figure 1 represents a front view of a tubular lantern with the air-chamber in section. Fig. 2 is a horizontal section looking downward, taken on the line x x of Fig. 3; and Fig. 3 is a front view of the air-chamber detached.

Like letters of reference made use of in the several figures indicate like parts.

General Description.

A is the oil-pot, B the burner of the lantern, and C the vertical wall of the air-chamber, resting in an annular groove, a, upon the top of the oil-pot, which groove facilitates the soldering of the wall C to said top. D is the cone, the base of which is made to fit over the upper edge of the wall C. E E are the air-tubes entering the sides of the air-chamber through the wall C. This vertical wall is stamped or drawn out of a flat piece of tin by appropriate machinery, and has the top and bottom open, with the top edge slightly beveled or rounded inward, as at b, for the greater ease of adjusting the cone to its place, and apertures e e are cut in opposite sides of the said wall to receive the tubes E E, which are soldered in place. By this construction the parts accurately fit one another and are interchangeable—the parts of one lantern for those of another—an advantage not easily overestimated in a large factory.

Claim.

Having thus fully described my invention, what I claim, and desire to secure by Letters Patent, is—

The vertical cylindrical wall C of the air-chamber of a tubular lantern, when stamped from a continuous sheet of metal, as shown and described, and for the purposes specified.

J. S. DENNIS.

Witnesses:
  JOHN W. MUNDAY,
  HEINR. F. BRUNS.

JOSEPH S. DENNIS.

Tubular Lantern.

No. 123,981.   Patented Feb. 27, 1872.

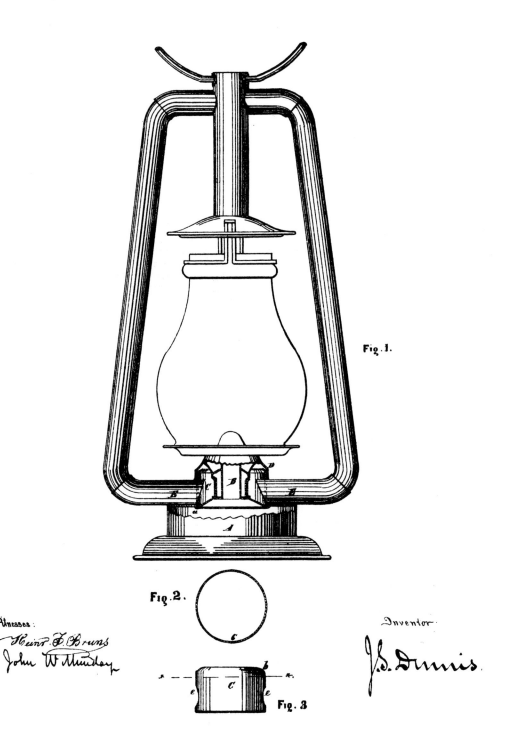

Fig.1.

Witnesses:

Heinr. F. Bruns

John W. Munday

Inventor

J. S. Dennis

Fig.2.

Fig.3.

119,518

UNITED STATES PATENT OFFICE.

JAMES J. HULL AND JOSEPH KAUFMAN, OF BROOKLYN, NEW YORK.

IMPROVEMENT IN LANTERNS.

Specification forming part of Letters Patent No. 119,518, dated October 3, 1871.

To all whom it may concern:

Be it known that I, JAMES J. HULL and JOSEPH KAUFMAN, both of the city of Brooklyn, county of Kings, and State of New York, have invented certain Improvements in Portable Lanterns, of which the following is a specification:

This invention relates to that class of lanterns which is used in the hand or for a portable light; and the improvement consists chiefly in the addition to other well-known devices of two reflectors or diffusers of the light, so constructed and arranged relatively to the burners and to each other as that the space around the lantern may be better illuminated than heretofore done.

Figure 1 represents a side elevation of the lantern complete, with the handle elevated, ready for being lifted. Fig. 2 is a vertical section through the center of the lantern.

Like letters refer to like parts.

A A is the base for receiving the burning-fluid in the lamp B, upon the top of which is the burner C, mounted in the usual manner, and provided with a chimney, D, as shown in the drawing. At the upper end of said chimney is a protector, E, of wire-gauze or perforated plate, to prevent the wind from acting against the draught and exterior. To this is a shield, F, to protect the hand or fingers from the heat of the chimney. Said upper parts are held or kept in position by the frame-work of wire or ribs of tin G G, which connects the base with the top, as shown in Figs. 1 and 2. H is the handle by which the lantern is carried, only shown in Fig. 1. At I I is a cylindrical shield of glass, like a shade commonly used around gas-burners, for keeping off the wind and rain from the chimney D and from the burner at C. Our improvement consists chiefly, however, in the introduction of two reflectors, as at L and M, which are made of any material that will reflect light readily, as planished tin, silvered glass,

or brass, acording to the cost and convenience of the user. These reflectors are placed in such a proximity to the burner, and relatively to each other, as to greatly diffuse the light from the burner and produce in some degree the effect of a head-light used on locomotives, but entirely around the burner. The lower one of said reflectors, as at L, is placed a little below the top of the burner, its crown being sufficiently far below the flame as that the light can fall upon it and be thrown outward and upward at whatever the incident angle may be. The other reflector or diffuser is placed with its reflecting focus downward to catch the light from the flame at the top of the burner; but the sides of said reflector are so inclined as not to catch the reflected rays from the lower reflector, or, at least, to any considerable extent, so that two reflectors act independently of each other, and yet both in combination with the burner, to produce the best results in giving light to a great distance. Of course, whatever rays are reflected from the inner surface of the shade I I will be again reflected by the surface at M M and thrown outward and downward; but the principal object of the two reflectors is to throw the rays from the flame outward and independently of each other, as may be readily seen by drawing the proper incident and reflecting angles from the top of the burner at or about where the center of the greatest light is produced.

Having thus described our invention, we claim—

As an article of manufacture, the lantern as described, for the purposes set forth.

JAMES J. HULL.
JOS. KAUFMAN.

Witnesses:
GEO. W. BENNETT,
BOYD ELIOT.

HULL & KAUFMAN'S

Improvement in Lamps

No. 119,518.   Patented Oct. 3, 1871.

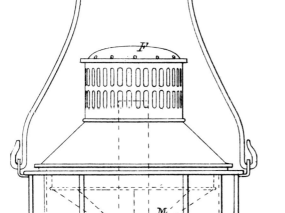
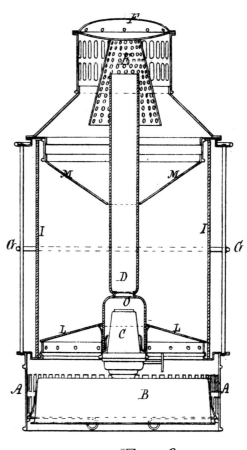

Fig. 1   *Fig. 2*

L. H. Gano   *Witness*   *James F. Hull*
N. Dollard.   *Jno. Kaufman*

                                      Inventor.

123,980

UNITED STATES PATENT OFFICE.

JOSEPH S. DENNIS, OF CHICAGO, ILLINOIS.

IMPROVEMENT IN TUBULAR LANTERNS.

Specification forming part of Letters Patent No. 123,980, dated February 27, 1872.

Specification describing certain Improvements in the Construction of Tubular Lanterns, invented by JOSEPH S. DENNIS, of Chicago, in the county of Cook and State of Illinois.

This invention relates to the method of constructing the joints between the vertical side tubes and the horizontal upper and lower tubes of the well-known "tubular lantern," whereby much labor and expense are saved in the manufacture of said lantern, and a stronger and better joint produced. And the invention consists in curving, by any of the well-known processes, the ends of the tin tubes to be joined, and inserting one end within the other, whereby but a single circular seam is left to be closed by solder.

The drawing represents an elevation of a tubular lantern containing my improvement, one of the joints being partially cut away to exhibit the method of joining. In the said drawing, A A represent the side tubes; B B, the upper horizontal tubes; and C C, the lower horizontal tubes.

It is desirable, in this style of lantern, that the joints between these tubes should be curved, both on account of the more graceful appearance of the lantern, and because of the more important fact that the curved joint allows an easier passage for the air; heretofore this curved portion of the tube has been made by stamping it out of tin in two halves, which were soldered together and then soldered to the tubes, making four seams to close by solder.

In the present invention, both ends of the side tubes A A are slightly curved, and the outer ends of the tubes B B C C also curved, so that the joint is formed by inserting one tube within the other, with a sufficient lap, as shown in the drawing, leaving only a single circular seam, a, which is soldered up, and the joint is complete.

Claims.

Having thus fully described my invention, what I claim, and desire to secure by Letters Patent, is—

The curved joint hereinbefore described for the tubes of tubular lanterns, made by curving the ends of the tubes and inserting one within the other, as specified and shown.

J. S. DENNIS.

Witnesses:
JOHN W. MUNDAY,
HEINR. F. BRUNS.

JOSEPH S. DENNIS.
Tubular Lantern.

No. 123,980.   Patented Feb. 27, 1872.

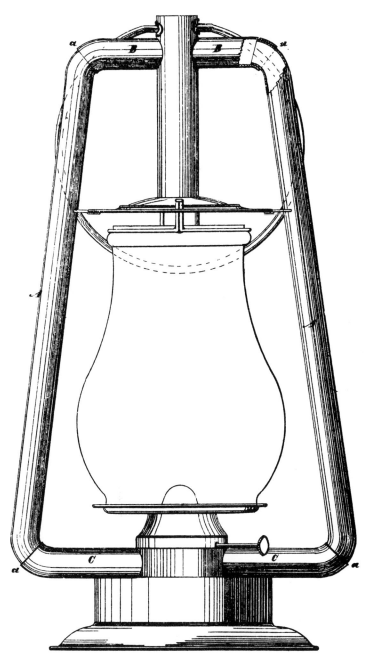

Witnesses: Inventor:

Hiar. F. Bums.

John W Munday   *J.S. Dennis.*

The Little Gem Lantern (Skaters) made by The Defiance Lantern & Stamping Co., Rochester, NY. Clear glass globe, 2 7/8" dia. brass base, 7" tall.

$100+

"Blue Grass Air Pilot" barn lantern, clear glass that reads (No. 30), by Belknap Hdware & Mfg. Co., Louisville, KY. 7 1/2" dia. base, 13 1/4" tall.

$20+

Bat (BS 3143) orange with three red reflector type lens, 5 1/2" sq. base, 15" tall (including hanger).

$40+

Dewey Mill Tubular F.O.
Dewey Co. Makers, Boston,
clear glass, 7 1/2" dia. base,
13 1/4" tall.
$150+

Dietz "Victor" barn lantern, N.Y., U.S.A.,
clear glass globe, 14" tall, 6" dia. base.
$100+

Dietz (New York, U.S.A.) Acme Inspectors Lamp, clear glass has reflective glare
guard and hood, 6 1/2" dia. base, 14" tall.
$50+

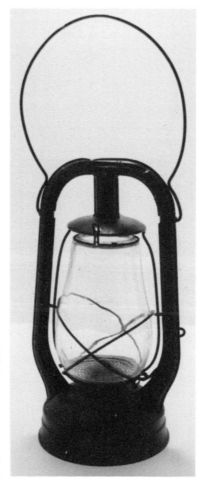

Dietz Monarch streamline model barn lantern, clear globe, New York, 6 1/2" dia. base, 13 1/2" tall.
$20+

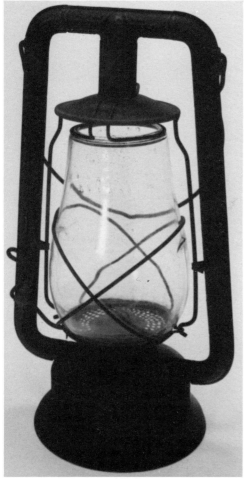

Dietz Monarch barn lantern, clear glass globe, 6" dia. base, 14" tall.
$85+

Dietz "Clipper" marine lantern, amber colored glass, 6" dia. base, 13 1/4" tall.
$35+

Dietz "Comet" barn lantern, clear glass, Syracuse, N.Y., 4_{1/2}" dia. base, 8_{1/2}" tall.

$10+

Dietz No. 2 D-Lite barn lantern, clear lens, New York, 6_{1/2}" dia. base, 13_{1/2}" tall.

$30+

Dietz No. 2 large Fount D-lite, New York, U.S.A., clear glass globe, 7_{3/4}" dia. base, 15_{1/4}" tall.

$30+

Dietz Sport, last pat. date Feb 10, 1914, N.Y., 3" dia. base, 8" tall.
$75+

Dietz "Little Giant" contractors lantern, 70 hour fount cap, amber lens, New York, 7½" dia. base, 12" tall.
$20+

Dietz No. 30 "Little Wizard" barn lantern, has back glare guard and reflector, clear glass, 6" dia. base, 11½" tall.
$30+

Dietz "Scout" last pat. date 2-10-1914, gun metal gray with clear lens, 3" dia. base, 7½" tall.
$75+

Dietz "Night Watch" contractors lantern, Red Fresnel Globe, Syracuse, N.Y., 6½" dia. base, 8¼" tall.
$35+

Dietz Eureka carriage or automobile lantern, 3" dia. base, 7½" tall.
$65+

Elgin barn lantern, dark amber globe, 7" dia. base, 14" tall.
$30+

Camlox No. 2 C.B. barn lantern, Embury Mfg. Co., Warsaw, N.Y., U.S.A., tin with copper top and bottom, 6 1/2" dia. base, 14" tall.
$75+

Embury Manufacturing Co., No. 40 "Traffic Gard", Warsaw, New York, U.S.A. Blue globe, 8" dia. base, 7 3/4" tall.
$50+

Little Defiance No. 1 barn lantern, made by the Embury Mfg. Co., Warsaw, N.Y. Clear glass globe, 6" dia. base, 11 1/2" tall.

$30+

Embury Mfg. Co., "Little Air Pilot", Warsaw - N.Y. - U.S.A., amber lens, 6 1/2" dia. base, 11 1/4" tall.

$30+

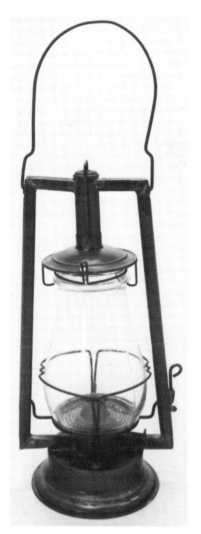

Ham's "Clipper" barn lantern, Model No. O, clear glass, 6" dia. base, 14" tall.

$150+

Hercules barn lantern, amber lens,
7 1/2" dia. base, 13 1/2" tall.
$40+

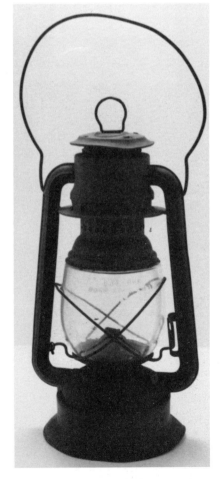

Ham's Advance, Rochester, N.Y.,
green with clear globe, 6 1/2" dia.
base, 14" tall.
$50+

Hibbard Spencer Bartlett & Co.,
O.V.B. No. 2 barn lantern, Chicago
clear glass, 6 1/2" dia. base, 14 1/2" tall.
$30+

Koehler Mfg. Co., Miner's Safety Lantern, Marlboro, Mass., made of aircraft aluminum, 3$1/2$" dia. base, 9$1/2$" tall.

$75+

Buckeye No. 2 barn lantern, C.B. The [.] Co., Warren, Ohio, pat. Jan 17, 1911. Amber globe, 6$1/2$" dia. base, 15" tall.

$40+

Hibbard Spencer Bartlett & Co. No. 2, Chicago, IL U.S.A., 7" dia. base, 14$1/2$" tall.

$25+

Paull's No. 0, last patent date June 30, 1909, green with amber globe, 7" dia. base, 13" tall.
$40+

Montgomery Ward "Wards Better Lantern", clear globe, 7 1/2" dia. base, 13" tall.
$30+

Paull's Leader, large fount No. 2, clear glass globe, 7 1/2" dia. base, 15" tall.
$35+

Regal No.0 barn lantern, amber globe, 6³/4" dia. base, 14" tall.

$30+

Rayo No. 82 "Cold Blast" barn lantern, clear glass tin with brass bottom made in U.S.A., 6³/4" dia. base, 15¹/2" tall.

$50+

"Norleigh Diamond" barn lantern clear glass, made by Shapleigh Hardware, St. Louis, U.S.A., 7¹/4" dia. base, 13¹/2" tall.

$25+

The Warren Stamping Co., Warren, OH. U.S.A. "Sta-Lite" No. 2 C. B., clear glass globe, 7 3/4" dia. base, 14" tall.
$30+

Van Camp No. 6 Supreme, gun metal grey with clear globe, 6 1/2" dia. base, 14" tall.
$30+

Van Camp No. 180 Air Pilot, clear globe, 7 1/2" dia. base, 12 1/2" tall.
$30+

The Wolf Safety Lamp Company, brass and iron miner's flame safety lamp, N.Y. USA, 3 1/4" dia. base, 11 1/2" tall.
$100+

British made ship's lantern, brass and copper constructed, 6" sq. base, 15" tall.
$190+

Barn Lantern, green painted with brass fuel cap and wick adjustment screw made in Great Britian, clear globe, 5" dia. base, 15" tall.
$50+

Fuer Hand No. 75 Atom, green with clear globe, made in Germany, 3" dia. base, 6$1/2$" tall.
$40+

German made carbide gas lantern, metal with brass inside's (H. Gillet) sides open to light gas, 3$3/4$" x 3" base, 8" tall (to top of lantern).
$75+

Nier Feurhand (Firehand) model no. 275, made in Germany, original clear glass globe, 4$1/2$" dia. base, 9$3/4$" tall.
$50+

Skater's lantern, brass top and bottom, clear glass globe, 3" dia. base, 7¼" tall.
$75+

Tin constructed skaters lamp, clear glass globe, 3" dia. base, 6¼" tall.
$60+

Pair of lanterns, one with blue lens the other with a red lens, 4" dia. base, 8½" tall.
$50+ each

Lamps.

ORDER BY PLATE AND LETTER   PLATE 59.

A.   Square Semaphore Lamp, N. Y. C. & H. R. R. R.

B.   Round Semaphore Lamp, one of the styles used on the Pennsylvania R. R.

C.   Distant Signal Lamp, Chicago & Northwestern R'y.

D.   Semaphore Lamp, 7" x 7" square, left-hand.

E.   Square Semaphore Lamp, sliding door.

F.   Square Semaphore Lamp, swing door.

G.   Round Semaphore Lamp, sliding door.

H.   Round Semaphore Lamp, swing door.

I. ⎫
   ⎬   These lamps are used either for switch targets or for our Electric Banner Signal.
J. ⎭   They are interchangeable and have the same socket.

K. ⎫   Pot Signal Lamps. – They differ principally in the method of fastening them to the
   ⎬
L. ⎭   pot signal.

M.   Main Line Semaphore Reflecting Lamp.

N.   Dwarf Signal Reflecting Lamp.

O.   Indicator Lamp.

P.   Illuminated Semaphore Lamp.

DURKEE'S NEW STYLE YACHT LIGHTS

Fig. 916-B

Fig. 917-B

Fig. 918-B

Polished Brass

Fresnal Glass

Fig. 916-B

Size Width	Glass Height	Height of Frame	Extreme Height	Price per Pair
4¾ in.	4¼ in.	· 9 in.	12 in.	$12.00

Fig. 917-B

Size Width	Glass Height	Height of Frame	Extreme Height	Price Each
4¾ in.	4¼ in.	9 in.	12 in.	$9.50

Fig. 918-B

Size Diameter	Glass Height	Height of Frame	Extreme Height	Price Each
4¾ in.	4¼ in.	9 in.	12 in.	$6.00

BOW LIGHTS

Galvanized and Brass

Fresnal Glass

No.	Size Glass Width Height	Height of Frame Inch	Extreme Height Inch	Width of Base Inch	Galvanized Each	Polished Brass Each
12	4¾ x 4¼	6⅝	10¼	5¼	$ 5.00	$ 6.75
13	4¾ x 4¼	8	11½	6	5.25	9.00
14	6 x 6	10	15	7½	5.75	9 50
15	6¾ x 6¾	10½	15½	7½	6.00	10.00
16	9 x 8	12½	21	10½	12.00	16.00

Plain Glass

No.	Size Glass Width Height	Height of Frame Inch	Extreme Height Inch	Width of Base Inch	Galvanized Each	Polished Brass Each
17	4½ x 4¼	6⅝	10¼	5¼	$4.50	$6.00
18	4½ x 4¼	8	11½	6	4.75	8.00
19	6¼ x 6½	10	15	7½	5.00	8.50
20	6¾ x 6¾	10	15½	7½	5.25	9.00

Fig. 917

SEA SHORE LANTERN

Polished Brass

Size of Glass	Height of Frame	Extreme Height	Each
4 x 5 in.	8 in.	11¼ in.	$6.50

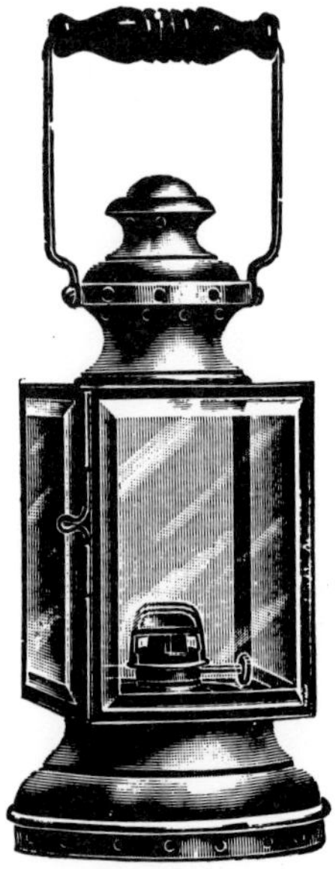

Fig. 922-A

REGULATION SHIP LIGHTS

English Pattern

Polished Brass or Copper

Fig. 916-A

Fig. 918-A

REGULATION MAST HEAD LIGHT

English Pattern

Polished Brass or Copper

No. 15-A	16-A
Size of Glass, in. 8x13	9x22
Height of Frame, in. 11	14
Extreme Height, " 16	20
Width of Base, " 11	14
Each.........$15.00	35.00

Fig. 917-A

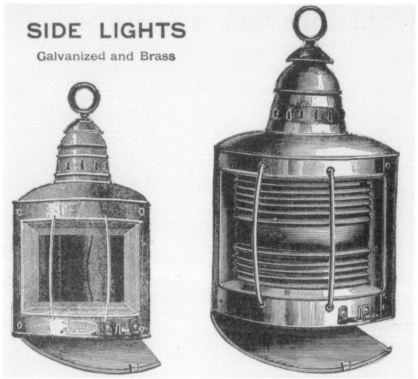

Fig. 915   **Fig. 916**

PLAIN GLASS
Fig. 915

No.	Size Glass Width	Height	Height of Frame	Extreme Height	Width of Base	Gal. Per Pair	Pol. Brass Per Pair
1	4¾	x 4¼	6½ inch	10¼ inch	6 inch	$3.75	$6.75
2	4¾	x 4¼	7⅜ "	11½ "	6½ "	5.00	9.00

DURKEE'S NEW STYLE LAUNCH LIGHTS
Polished Brass

Fig. 925-A

Size of Glass	Height of Frame	Extreme Height	Each
4 x 4 in.	7¼ in	11¼ in	$10.50

Fig. 924-A

Diameter Glass	Height of Frame	Extreme Height	Each
2¼ in.	6½ in.	10 in.	$9.00
3 "	8¼ "	12 "	10.50

NAVY LANTERN OR ANCHOR LIGHT
Plain Glass. Galvanized and Brass

Diam. of Globe	Height of Globe	Height of Lantern	Diam. of Base	Galv. per Dozen	Pol. Brass per poz.
5 in.	6½ in.	12 in.	6 in.	$15.75	$34.50
Without Bottom...... .. ..13.50					27.00
With Ruby Globe, Extra..... ....Per doz.					8.00
" Green " " .... "					6.00
" Blue " " ....·.·..... "					6.00

Fig. 919

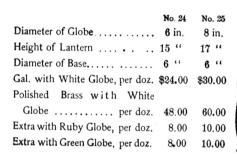

	No. 24	No. 25
Diameter of Globe........	6 in.	8 in.
Height of Lantern	15 "	17 "
Diameter of Base......	6 "	6 "
Gal. with White Globe, per doz.	$24.00	$30.00
Polished Brass with White Globe .... per doz.	48.00	60.00
Extra with Ruby Globe, per doz.	8.00	10.00
Extra with Green Globe, per doz.	8.00	10.00

Fig. 920

Galvanized and Brass

Fresnal Glass

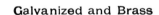

No.	Diam. of Glass Inch	Height of Glass Inch	Height of Frame Inch	Extreme Height Inch	Galvanized Each	Polished Brass Each
21	4¾	4¼	9½	14	$ 3.00	$ 5.00
22	6	5½	12	17¼	5.25	10.00
23	8½	7	13	21	10.50	15.00

With Ruby or Green Globes

No.	Galvanized Each	Polished Brass Each
21	$ 4.50	$ 6.50
22	7.00	11.75
23	13.50	18.00

Fig. 918

BABY SAILING LIGHTS

For Small Launches and Yachts

Galvanized and Brass

Fig. 916-C
Side

Fig. 917-C
Bow

Fig. 916-C
Side

Size Glass	Height of Frame	Extreme Height	Width of Base
3 in.	4⅝ in.	8¼ in.	4⅝ in.

Galvanized, each $2.50
Polished Brass, each 3.50

FIG. 916-D
Side

FIG. 917-D
Bow

FIG. 916-D
Side

Size Glass	Height of Frame	Extreme Height	Width of Base
3¼ x 3½ in.	4⅝ in.	8¼ in.	4⅝ in.

Galvanized, each $2.50
Polished Brass, each 3.50

BINNACLE LIGHTS

Polished Brass

Total Height	Diameter	Each
5 inches	1⅞ inches	$2.50
5½ "	2¾ "	3.00
6½ "	2¾ "	3.50

Fig. 928-A

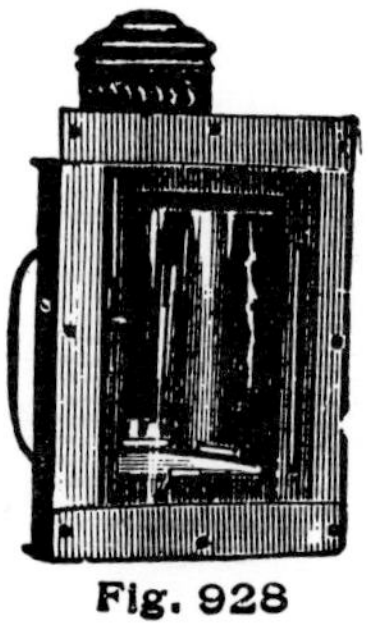

Fig. 928

Polished Brass

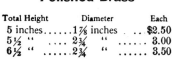

Size of Glass Clear	Height of Frame	Extreme Height	Width	Polished Brass Each
2½x3½ inch	4½ inch	8 inch	3½ inch	$2.50
3 x4½ inch	5½ inch	9 inch	4½ inch	3.00
4 x5¾ inch	7 inch	10¼ inch	5½ inch	3.50

MARITIME LANTERNS FROM 1909 CATALOG

COMBINATION LIGHTS

Fig. 924

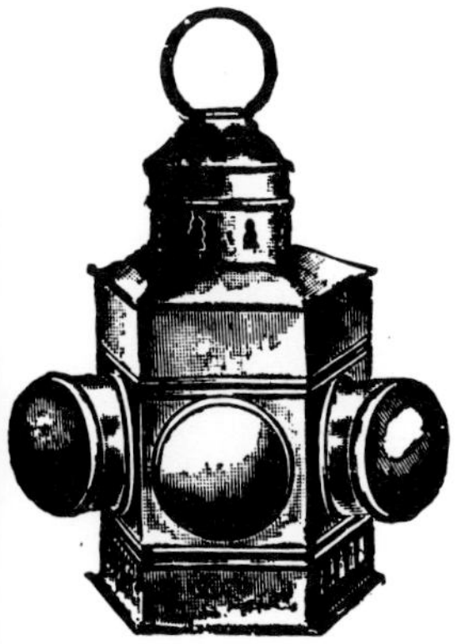

FOR LAUNCHES

With Red, White, and Green Bullseye Glasses. Galvanized and Brass

Diam. Glass	Height of Frame	Extreme Height	Width of Base	Galvanized Each	Polished Brass Each
2¼ in.	5½ in.	9 in.	5¼ in.	$5.00	6.50
8 "	6½ "	10½ "	7 "	6.00	7.50

FOR CATBOATS

With Red and Green Bullseye Glasses

Diam. Glass	Height of Frame	Extreme Height	Width of Base	Galvanized Each	Polished Brass Each
2¼ in.	5½ in.	9 in.	5¼ in.	$4.50	6.00
3 "	6½ "	10½ "	7 "	5.50	7.00

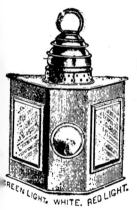

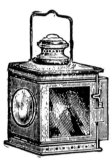

Fig. 926

COMBINATION LIGHTS

FOR CANOES

Galvanized and Brass

Size Glass	Height of Frame	Extreme Height	Width of Base	Galvanized Each	Polished Brass Each
4x4 in.	4½ in.	10 in.	5 in.	$6.00	7.50

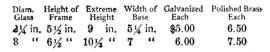

Fig. 925

COMBINATION LIGHTS

FOR LAUNCHES

Galvanized and Brass

Size Glass	Height of Frame	Extreme Height	Width of Base	Galvanized Each	Polished Brass Each
4x4 in.	5½ in.	9 in.	7 in.	$5 00	$6.50
4x4 "	6½ "	10½ "	7 "	6.00	7.50

Fig. 927

COMBINATION LIGHTS

Galvanized and Brass

FOR CATBOATS

Size of Glass Width Height	Height of Frame	Extreme Height	Width of Base	Galvanized Each	Polished Brass Each
4 x 5 in.	...7 in.	...10 in.	...7 in.	...$3.50	.....$6.00

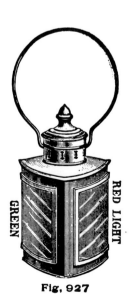

PRICING GUIDE

The current prices in this guide are for items in working condition only. These prices should only be used as a guide. They are not to set prices, which may vary from one region of the country to another. Dealer prices vary greatly and are affected by condition as well as demand. Neither the author nor the publisher assume responsibility for any losses or gains that might be a result of consulting this guide.

Page 9) top row (left to right)
500+, 600+
bottom row all 500+

Pg 10) all on page 500+

Pg 11) "Excelsior"- 500+ "Boat"- 700+
"Sugar House"- 750+
"Street"- 500+

Pg 12) top row (left to right)
200+, 300+, 200+

Pg 13) top row all 400+
bottom row #15- 175+
#17- 200+ #634- 750+

Pg 14) top row all 250+
bottom row #18- 200+
#354- 150+ #35- 150+
#40- 200+

Pg 15) top row all 300+
bottom row all 350+

Pg 16) top row (left to right)
200+, 500+
middle row all 150+
bottom row (left to right)
400+, 450+

Pg 17) #7- 400+, #8- 150+, #258- 200+
#211- 350+, #212- 350+
#2- 200+, #50- 100+

Pg 18) Dietz side lift- 150+
Dietz crystal- 175+
Dietz US Brass- 350+
#18- 150+, Dietz safety- 200+
Dietz square lift- 300+
Dietz Buckeye- 150+
Dietz tubular driving- 100+
Dietz tubular hunting- 150+
Dietz new form- 350+
wire bottom- 150+

Pg 19) Dietz tubular driving- 100+
Dietz tubular hunting - 150+
Dietz new farm - 350+
10 inch square- 400+
Dietz sq. station lamp- 400+
Dietz RR lantern- 150+
car inspectors lantern- 300+
police or dark- 300+
Dietz tubular side- 175+
Dietz searchlight- 200+
Dietz improved tubular- 400+
Dietz tubular hanging- 300+
Dietz corp. street lamp- 200+
Dietz #2 square- 200+
Dietz #3 globe- 300+

Pg 20) wire bottom RR- 150+
tin bottom RR- 175+
Dietz conductor- 150+
square lift or star- 200+
side lift or victor- 150+
Dietz crystal- 175+
Dietz #1B- 150+
Dietz junior cold blast- 100+
Dietz safety tubular- 200+
Dietz square lift brass- 300+
Dietz buckeye or #13- 150+
Dietz #0- 425+
cold blast dash lamp- 60+
Dietz Junior cold blast- 50+

Pg 21) Dietz monarch- 65+
Dietz junior- 70+
Dietz Blizzard- 50+
Special Blizzard- 35+
Dietz US lantern- 125+
union driving lamp- 200+
night drivers lamp- 225+

Pg 22) blizzard dash- 375+
conductors lantern- 150+
Dietz #6 railroad- 150+
ACMC inspectors- 175+
Dietz improved vulcan- 150+

Pg 23) top row (left to right) 75+, 15+
mid row (left to right) 50+, 20+
bot row (left to right) 100+, 35+

Pg 24) Dietz monarch hot blast- 75+
Dietz Little Wizard- 15+
Dietz Royal- 30+
Dietz regular D-lite- 20+
Dietz Blizzard- 20+
Dietz large D-lite- 20+
Dietz Junior- 20+
Dietz standard- 45+

Pg 25) top row (left to right) 40+, 35+
mid row (left to right) 40+, 25+
bot row (left to right) 100+, 50+

Pg 26) Dietz junior wagon- 35+
Dietz #2 De-lite- 50+
Dietz special #2 blizzard- 20+
Dietz boy scout- 75+
Wonder Junior- 45+

Pg 27) Little Wizard- 15+
Dietz rooster- 35+
Dietz #2 large- 25+

Pg 30) Adlake reliable- 200+
#39 double guard- 200+

Pg 31) Adlake reliable- 200+
#39 wire guard- 200+

Pg 32) #11 double guard- 200+
queen closed bottom- 250+
queen open bottom- 250+
pullman- 275+

Pg 33) #7 steamboat- 300+
tri-color lamp- 200+
police or watch- 225+

Pg 34) #39 outside wick raiser- 175+

Pg 35) #90 wood bail- 175+
#91 combination- 150+

Pg 36) #199- 500+, #40- 400+

Pg 37) all on page 200+

Pg 40) all on page 50+

Pg 41) #33 tail lamp- 300+, #63- 100+

Pg 42) all on page 125+

Pg 43) all on page 100+

Pg 44) #169- 125+, # 169 1/2- 100+

Pg 45) #206- 150+, all others 125+

Pg 46) all on page 110+

Pg 47) #219- 100+, all others 150+

Pg 48) #3- 110+, #6- 300+

Pg 49) #7- 300+, #9- 100+

Pg 50) #10- 100+, #81- 125+

Pg 51) #140- 125+, #107- 500+

Pg 52) #158- 100+, #173- 225+

Pg 53) #180- 125+, #187- 150+

Pg 54) all on page 125+

Pg 55) #207- 200+, #9- 110+

Pg 56) #82- 125+, #130- 100+

Pg 57) tub. station- 250+, #15- 300+

Pg 58) all on page 200+

Pg 59) #203- 125+, #78- 150+

Pg 60) all on page 200+

Pg 61) all on page 200+

Pg 62) #190- 175+, #191- 150+

Pg 63) #275- 125+, #319- 80+

Pg 64) #175- 125+, #175 1/2- 100+

Pg 67) #294 porter- 100+
pet- 75+, #297 porter- 100+
#295 porter- 100+
#296 porter- 100+
all others 125+

Pg 68) Broadway- 350+
Manhattan- 400+
Universal- 175+
#424- 70+, Penn- 125+

Pg 69) #300- 80+, #301- 100+
#277 Cyclone- 300+
locomotive headlight-
all sizes- 600+

Pg 70) #278- all - **500+**

Pg 71) #425- 350+, #246- **50+**
#434- 40+, #431- **100+**
#433- **150+**
all others **200+**

Pg 72) #432- 175+, #428- **225+**
#429- 150+, #423- **225+**
#437- 50+, #438- **75+**
#440- 150+, #441- **150+**

Pg 73) #192- 500+, #198- pair **400+**
galvanized- pair **300+**
#407- pair **300+**
#197galvanized- pair **200+**
brass- pair **275+**
#194- pair **400+**
#195 galvanized- pair **200+**
brass- pair **300+**
galvan. plain glass- pair **175+**
brass plain glass- pair **275+**
#191- pair **600+**

Pg 74 #190- pair **600+**
#196- pair **300+**
#199- pair **175+**
#257- **150+**, ellis- **750+**

Pg 75) #211- **200+**, #212- **200+**
#213- **200+**, #214- **300+**
#215- **300+**, #216- **200+**

Pg 76) #202- **250+**, #203- **200+**
#204- **175+**, #205- **200+**
#207- **300+**, #206- **400+**

Pg 77) #220- **500+**, #241- **200+**
#208- **300+**, #209- **275+**
#276- **250+**

Pg 78) #468- **500+**, #242- **300+**
#193- **350+**

Pg 79) #219- **50+**, #201- **150+**
#266- **75+**, #189- **400+**
#210- **250+**

Pg 80) lamp lighter- **50+**, #255- **150+**
#425- **75+**, #217- **200+**
#218- **125+**, #299- **100+**
#258- **250+**, #439- **150+**

Pg 81) Peerless #2- **15+ each**
standard tubular- **25+ each**
H.B. & H.- **100+ each**

Pg 82) top row (left to right)
35+, 40+, 30+
bot row (left to right)
40+, 50+, 60+

Pg 83) #140- **35+**, #180- **30+**
#230- **30+**, #220- **30+**
#250 (not shown)- **30+**

Pg 85) #11- **300+**, #4- **300+**
#6- **400+**, #10- **450+**

Pg 86) #9 hanging lamp- **200+**
#9 street lamp- **200+**
10 inch traction- **500+**
#40- **150+**, #2- **40+**

#12- **150+**, #2- **40+**
#0- **40+**, #15- **45+**
#17- **50+**

Pg 87) #0 oval tube- **125+**
#0 mill tubular- **145+**

Pg 88) #300 galvanized- pair **100+**
brass- pair **175+**
#301 galvanized- **75+**
brass- **100+**
($10- $15 less for fresnel lens)

Pg 89) #200 galvanized- pair **100+**
brass- pair **150+**
#201 galvanized- pair **50+**
brass- pair **80+**
#202 galvanized- pair **60+**
brass- pair **125+**
($10- $15 less for fresnel lens)

Pg 90) dark lantern #10- **60+**
dark lantern #20 (not shown)- **70+**
leader tubular- **80+**
side spring oval tube - **80+**
clipper lift - **80+**

Pg 91) gem driving lamp - **50+**
casey lantern - **75+**
cold blast tin - **60+**
clipper tubular - **50+**

Pg 92) lightweight - **75+** Jim Dandy - **75+**
banner - **80+** I.C. - **100+**
Everlit - **100+** Dietz - **80+**

Pg 93) all on page - **100+**

Pg 94) M & W - **100+**
ham's diamond - **125+**
20th Century - **100+**
searchlight - **175+**
x-rays - **100+**

Pg 95) early tole wrislet - **550+**
six sided presentation -
(very rare piece) - **5,000+**
both Fire King lanterns -
between **300-400+**

Pg 96) chief's lantern polished brass
by Peter Gray - **500+**
wrist lantern - **350+**
brass chief's lantern with
large bail - **400+**
ham lantern - **200+**
Dietz Fire Queen - **200+**
pair of Dietz lanterns - **400+ each**

Pg 97) top row (left to right) - **400+, 800+**
bot. row (left to right) - **800+, 400+**

Pg 98-117) original patent diagrams are
$35 each in mint condition
(depending on year of patent &
condition of paper)

Pg 118-133) values of lanterns on these
pages are under the
individual picture

Pg 135) all on page are **200-400+**

Pg 136) top row - all **200+**
bot. row (left to right)
150+, 300+

Pg 137) all on page **300+**

Pg 138) all on page **250+**

Pg 139) #919 - **200+**, #920 - **250+**
#918 - **200+**

Pg 140) top two rows -
galvanized - **40+**
brass - **50+**
#928-A - **75+**, #928 - **200+**

Pg 141) #924 - **200+** #926 - **350+**
#925 - **300+** #927 - **250+**

Pg 142) #1 & #2 - **museum stock**
#3 & #4 - **rare**
#5 - **500+**, #6 - **400+**
#7 - **250+**, #8 - **400+**
#9 - **500+**, #10 - **400+**
#11 - **300+**, #12 - **300+**
#13 - **250+**, #14 - **200+**
#15 - **200+**

INDEX